GREEN BANANAS

The Wisdom of Father Bill Atkinson

BY

STEVE MCWILLIAMS

EDITED BY
MARY ELLEN FATTORI

HARROWOOD BOOKS

NEWTOWN SQUARE, PENNSYLVANIA

The publisher and author would like to thank The Father Bill Atkinson Foundation for providing photographs of Father Bill, his family and friends; many of which appear in the final chapter *Epilogue and Reminiscences*.

For information about The Father Bill Atkinson Foundation, visit: www.fatherbillatkinson.org

We would also like to thank Mary Moody for her help in finding and identifying photographs of Father Bill and his family.

Hardcover Edition
ISBN-13   978-0-915180-44-8
ISBN-10   0-915180-44-8

Trade Paperback Edition
ISBN-13   978-0-915180-45-5
ISBN-10   0-915180-45-6

LIBRARY OF CONGRESS CATALOGING-IN-PUBLICATION DATA

McWilliams, Steve (Stephen Thomas), 1954-

Green bananas : the wisdom of Father Bill Atkinson / by Steve McWilliams ; edited by Mary Ellen Fattori. -- Trade paperback ed.

  p. cm.

ISBN 978-0-915180-44-8 (hardcover) -- ISBN 978-0-915180-45-5 (pbk.)

1. Atkinson, Bill (William), d. 2006. 2. Catholic Church--Pennsylvania--Philadelphia--Clergy--Biography. 3. Quadriplegics--Pennsylvania--Philadelphia--Biography. 4. Fattori, Mary Ellen. I. Title.

BX4705.A7675M39 2010

271'.402--dc22

[B]

                                2010043630

10 9 8 7 6 5 4 3 2 1

HARROWOOD BOOKS
3943 N PROVIDENCE ROAD
NEWTOWN SQUARE, PA 19073
800-747-8356

PRINTED IN THE U.S.A.

Dedicated to all of the disabled persons
with whom I have worked over the years.

Thank you for the education
...I needed it!

CONTENTS

Foreword by Jim Murray ix

Acknowledgements xiii

Introduction 17

Chapter 1   Exposition Near the End 23

Chapter 2   Basic Training 39

Chapter 3   The Strength of Others 51

Chapter 4   Lemons and Lemonade 69

Chapter 5   Bird's Eye View 81

Chapter 6   Doubting Thomas 95

Chapter 7   The Ninth Life 105

Chapter 8   Looking Back 117

Chapter 9   The Saint Thing 125

Chapter 10   Some Good Bill Talking 131

Chapter 11   Adieu and Words To Remember 145

Chapter 12   Epilogue and Reminiscences (and photos) 157

FOREWORD

BY JIM MURRAY

THIS IS NOT JUST A BOOK...IT'S A PRAYER. THE STORY SPEAKS FOR ITSELF AND will mean something to each person in a very personal way.

The nuns taught us in Catholic school there are three kinds of prayer: praise, thanksgiving, and petition. Irish guys can't handle praise. It is part of our training. Father Bill and Steve are perfect examples. Thanksgiving is not just a Thursday in November, but that most important reminder to be thankful for the ordinary things in life. One of the saints provided a great quote: *Doing ordinary things in God's name makes them truly extra ordinary.* And petition. Sometimes, the things we pray for change in an instant. Father Bill's accident changed his life— and all those who read this book—forever.

In a previous life, I was the General Manager of an NFL football team, and if I would compare this story—the way it is written and what it says—this book is a first-round draft pick. If I were comparing it to other works, I would say it is somewhere between St. Augustine's *Confessions* and Rick Warren's *It's a Purposeful Life.*

The journey chronicled in this book is both physical and spiritual. For Steve, he volunteered and spent several decades taking care of some of Father Bill's basic needs—dressing him and getting him ready for the day. They did not develop a deep friendship or intimate sharing, until their relationship changed during the collaboration on this book. The friendship first took a meaningful turn when Father Bill asked Steve to come over and watch a basketball game on ESPN. At the end of the game, Father Bill said, *"Would you like to read a poem I wrote?"* And when you read his poems and consider his life, you read them slowly, and each line, each word will bring you some tears and cheers.

The interesting style of the book comes from the fact that both Steve and Father Bill are teachers. The topics that they talk about are from deep waters: What it means to be a teacher? What about death? What kind of an impact do you have on the people you teach? What do you learn? What do you know of God?

The miracle of Father Bill's paralyzed body, his totally nimble mind, and the maestro questioner, Steve—like an orchestra—find a perfect harmony. If they were doing the rosary, they would touch on both the most sorrowful and joyful mysteries in the same movement.

The heart and soul of this book live in Father Bill's *faith, family, friends* and *friars*. To every question and probing insight that Steve brings to the table, those four are part of the answer. As I wrote earlier, the Irish humor, the heavy topics, the journey that both men take in telling this story, form the soul of the book. In a personal way, the book is a life changer for me and it compliments and reminds me of the greatness of hard working moms and dads, brothers and sisters, and teachers in school.

Recently, I read a beautiful reflection and it mentioned that the word *silent* and the word *listen* have exactly the same letters. Steve confesses that he hates long silences and Father Bill really didn't have an option. But as their journeys came together, I think they both heard in the silence and in their hearts how much they were the same.

What I am struggling to say is summed up in the beautiful hymn:

You Are Mine.
I will come to you in the silence
I will lift you from all your fear
You will hear My voice
I claim you as My choice
Be still and know I am here

And I guess if I were to sum up both these men, there is a quote from St. Francis de Sale which is my favorite: ***"Nothing is so strong as gentleness, and nothing is so gentle as real strength."***

— JIM MURRAY
Former General Manager, Philadelphia Eagles
and Founder of Ronald McDonald House

ACKNOWLEDGEMENTS

NEVER DID I EXPECT TO FINISH THIS BOOK AND WRITE AN ACKNOWLEDGEMENT section. But now that I have, I should thank several people. There were several key people who supported me throughout this effort.

First and foremost, I have to thank my family. My wife Cathy, and my children, Julia, Janet, Stephen, Daniel, and James. Cathy, you've put up with lots of crazy ideas of mine over the years but I hope this one is worthwhile. Thanks for the faithful , unwavering support and love you display daily. Hey kids, you were wondering what I was doing on a laptop every night for a year? Here it is, and thanks for your patience when I wasn't paying attention to the nightly, "Hey, Dad…yo, Dad…Dad are you listening?"

I must thank my parents, Phyllis and Jim, who taught me to be a participant, not a spectator. My deceased father hated to have his children sitting idly, doing nothing. Their message and example taught me to live and care about things with great passion. Get involved in something was their counsel. I probably would have never said yes to the first request to help Bill, if they hadn't drummed into me the ability to never say no to helping another. Hey, but that's a good thing, right?

I would not be writing an acknowledgement section if it were not for the efforts of my dear friend Mary Ellen Fattori. Besides editing the book and being a terrific English professor, Mary Ellen was a constant supporter, cheerleader, and believer in this project. She handled my "Woody Allen-like" neuroses like Sigmund Freud. Thank you for the regular Tuesday morning sessions where sometimes we worked on the book, but most of the time using Bill's words as a jump off point for long philosophical and theological therapy sessions. All the commas and periods seem to be in the right places, but more importantly, you got my mind in the right place to complete this. Again, I express my deepest gratitude for your friendship.

Thank you Father Art Chappell, OSA for the encouragement, support, and patience throughout these past two years. Your positive energy and love for Bill were great motivators. Without your green light, this would have stayed on the shelf.

Soon after Bill's death, his cousin Mary Moody discovered that I had been interviewing Bill and helping him with his poetry. Mary, who was very close to Bill, through phone conversations and email, kept on me to write this book. Mary, I think Bill worked through you to nudge me. Great nudging!

My publisher, Paul Nigel Harris, gets a shout out for being Paul Nigel Harris. Paul quickly became a great friend and mentor after reading the initial manuscript. Your insight, knowledge, and honesty are great gifts. Thanks for recognizing that Bill Atkinson is a great subject and bringing this to fruition.

Aside from thanking those who influenced, helped, persuaded with the book, there are many other folks I met on my journey with Bill who have inspired me to be a better person. Rich Heron, whom I mention in the book, is a great human being. It's no accident there's "hero" in Heron. I've met few people in my life who live their beliefs everyday. Rich, I've met few people who have made me say, "I wish I could be more like him." Thanks for your example!

To Bill's family, you don't need me to tell you that you were the reason that Bill kept living. Your loyalty to him was remarkable and he never failed to bring it up in every conversation. His love for you was his favorite topic. I hope I've done well by your brother.

To all of the many Bonner boys and non-Bonner boys who helped with Bill over the years. You were great caretakers and great friends to Bill.

There were many, many people who did much more than I in being there for Bill, day in and day out for 41 years. I don't remember everyone's name but Chris, Mike, Tim, you pop in first, and you represent the best of a Bonner education. Fellow teachers and friends of Bill, he cherished his Bonner colleagues.

To all of Bill's Augustinian brothers, he was proud to be one of you. After his accident, many of you took the responsibility of "brother" to new levels. Bill was fortunate to be a member of a caring, compassionate fraternity.

To all of the health care workers, in particular, the round-the-clock nurses, who cared for Bill in the last year of his life. In particular Gwen, who acted as gatekeeper when Bill became gravely ill. We're lucky you chose the right profession!

Lastly, I thank the disabled people to whom I'm related and those with whom I've worked at Villanova. My Aunt Mary Thompson has taught me the importance of looking past disability to see ability. Hopefully, this book will make a small contribututuion to the evolution of treating the disabled as full members of our society.

INTRODUCTION

THIS BOOK IS A TRIBUTE TO A FRIEND, A DEAD FRIEND. IT IS MY FIRST ATTEMPT at writing such a tribute. I proceed with caution. Throughout my life, I have written creatively as both playwright and screenwriter. For some reason, these writing forms come easily to me. Maybe because I'm in control; I'm making it up as I go. However, a book, this book in particular, differs greatly from a play or a movie. Right from the start, writing about my friend comes with pressure. Accurate portrayal is essential.

Over my life I've written quite a few fictional works, some with moderate success, some occupying a landfill near the Meadowlands. Yet, my friend was real, and my experiences did happen and were unusual, even life altering. And so, as I begin to type away, I lose some of the cushion that creative writing offers me.

Initially, I resisted this project. I worry constantly. So when I began thinking about this book, I instantly began to worry—and put things off—and question myself. During deep moments of uncertainty, I doubted my ability to accurately portray my friend or do justice to his memory. What if I don't get him right? I'm not even sure I knew him well enough to write about him. Others knew him much better. In fact, there were long stretches in our relationship where I didn't think we were friends at all. As a result, I desire no competition for a place in the hierarchy of his friends or criticism for not fully capturing the perfect memorial. I only promise to try and reinforce what others know to be true about him. With pangs of timidity rumbling inside me, I proceed. I'm taking my chances, writing down my thoughts, but in my small way, I will honor my friend.

Father William Atkinson was an ordained priest. He was also a quadriplegic. He died four years ago and we had an odd relationship that I chronicled over a long period of time. Father Bill was also a puzzling figure in my life. Every Monday and Wednesday, for over 25 years, I helped dress, feed, and get him off to work. During these many mornings, we shared a strange, uncomfortable intimacy. I'm sure there are many people, family members or nurses, who perform similar functions for other quadriplegics. But for me, dressing a paralyzed man put me in a not-so-ordinary situation.

Although there evolved a forced familiarity over time, for most of our years together, I never felt any warmth or closeness to or from Father Bill, at least not until shortly before his death. It was only a relatively brief time before he died that I learned we were true friends. It took over two decades to mutually admit that we had become close friends. Today I count him as one of the most influential people in my life.

I once described my relationship to Father Bill as being disciple-like. The term embarrassed him, and he was taken aback by it. But happily, I was able to tell him what I thought of him before he died. In hindsight, that was a valuable life lesson for me. Too often in life, I keep my mouth shut and don't speak up. I'm afraid to express what I'm feeling for whatever reason. I recall several regrettable relationships in my life where I failed to tell those persons how much I loved them or what they meant to me. Those omissions still follow and trouble me. Luckily with Bill, I'm off the hook on that account

My participation in his care started as an awkward obligation but grew into a precious gift. Our meeting and subsequent relationship was unintentional. Neither one sought out the other nor did either of us work at developing a friendship. Initially, I was a clumsy, unskilled caretaker. Many days he would get angry with me and bark a snappy command. On those days, I'd ask myself why I bothered. I confess there were times throughout the years that I wished I never became involved.

Many people who knew Father Bill described him as a quiet, holy man.

Even though I initially felt uncomfortable with him on a personal level, I did marvel at his courage, perseverance, and behemoth faith. It's not that others haven't turned lemons into lemonade, but Father Bill's journey was extraordinary, like Mother Teresa extraordinary, and worth sharing. A much wiser person than I once told me that great truths are revealed subtly and through experience. We only realize the profound after the fact. It takes a generation for icons to become icons. That's the sort of experience I had with Father Bill. It was during many reflective moments in the past four years, I have realized the profound after the fact.

A few weeks before Father Bill's death, I jokingly remarked that if there were life after death, could he possibly get word to me. I'd appreciate some kind of contact or sign that there was at least a nice parking spot waiting for me when I pass.

"Do me a favor;" I asked, "at least get in touch and let me know the weather's warm."

Chuckling, he responded, "I'm sure I'll be hanging around somewhere; pay close attention."

Now I might be going way out on a limb saying this, but since his death, I feel a strange, ongoing presence around me from time to time. Even as I pushed the book idea further back in my mind, he continued to urge me on to write it. No ghost, no voices. It's just that whenever I have paused or totally lost interest in this idea, mysteriously, something compelled me to return.

Sound overdramatic? Flat out nuts? You're right. Maybe I am. But something was at work, pushing me to write. Not a white light, no burning bush, but rather a real presence gnawing at me to complete this. Each time I walked away, Father Bill's impatient memory called to me saying,

"Knock it off; shut up and write!"

So I'm just going to let go and trust that it comes out well. Believe me—I don't want to do this book. It's Bill Atkinson working through me from the other side!

The title of this book is called *Green Bananas*. What do green bananas have to do with a quadriplegic priest? Several years ago, Villanova University granted Father Bill an honorary doctorate degree and asked him to speak at commencement. His response to this highly prestigious invitation was,

"I never buy green bananas."

University Vice President, Dr. Helen Lafferty, asked him to clarify what he meant by that expression. Father Bill replied,

"In my condition, I don't buy green bananas because I may not be alive by the time they ripen. Since my life is so day to day, I may not make it to the graduation ceremony, but if I'm alive, I'll be there."

When I told Dr. Lafferty that I was attempting a book about Bill, she insisted that I call it, *Green Bananas*. To her goes all the credit for the title. Her story struck me as the perfect metaphor for Bill's pragmatic, honest approach to his disability—and to life itself.

True to his word, Father Bill passed away soon after sharing this metaphor. His medical history always read like the *Physician's Desk Reference*. From bed sores to pneumonia to bone marrow infections, throughout his adult life, Father Bill defied the medical experts time and time again. Living as long as he did with a spinal cord injury surprised even the leading experts. It's rare for a quadriplegic to live into his sixties. Doctors and nurses marveled at how many times death knocked on Father Bill's door, only for him to graciously decline. Moment to moment suffering and pain were his lifelong companions. Yet he saw hope in every second.

In addition to paying tribute to a remarkable human being, I have a few other goals for this book. I genuinely hope that this collection of memories, co-authored in part by Father Bill himself, might serve as a practical spiritual guide for some readers. For those struggling with the tough existential questions about God and life's meaning, I hope my simple conversations with Father Bill provide some gentle reassurances about the power of God's love in which Father Bill believed so deeply. His words truly contain valuable lessons and reminders of the wisdom available to us all.

Also, since Father Bill was a quadriplegic this first hand experience might very well promote some useful awareness for those who do not always see or have the opportunity to know a disabled person. Who knows? Maybe this book might even inspire others to reach out and help in their communities, in particular to work for access and justice for the disabled community.

And so, with Father Bill's help, both then and now, I offer this humble portrait of a unique individual and the impact he had on me and everyone with whom he came in contact. He was uncommonly of another world.

—STEVE MCWILLIAMS
HAVERTOWN, PENNSYLVANIA
SEPTEMBER, 2010

CHAPTER 1

EXPOSITION NEAR THE END

FATHER WILLIAM ATKINSON, AUGUSTINIAN PRIEST, DIED ON SEPTEMBER 15TH, 2006. Sitting in my office that morning, I received a call from Rich Heron a former seminarian classmate of Bill who was also now his private nurse. Rich informed me that Bill had slipped into unconsciousness after a difficult two days. He asked if I wanted to come over to Bill's room to say a final goodbye. I declined. I didn't feel it was appropriate for me to be present as family and loved ones stood watch over him. In such a setting I felt like a relative stranger. Ironically, though, no one there knew what close friends we had become.

For that past year, I had been privately recording conversations with him that we planned on using in a book. It was an idea I had hoped to execute before his sickness cut short the plan. Two months prior to his death, however, he became too ill to speak. Faintly he whispered to me one day,

"Looks like you're going to have to finish this without me."

I walked into Bill's life long ago, October 20th, 1985, to be specific. On that day, my official first day on the job dressing Bill, I felt odd, uncomfortable, almost unwanted by the man I had agreed to help. It was a moment I easily could have walked away from and not felt guilty. With a new job and a new baby, there was just too much activity in my life. I certainly wasn't looking for volunteer opportunities. But a chance meeting with a friend of a friend had resulted in a request to help someone who had suffered a traumatic spinal cord injury.

Another commitment? At first I tried to opt out, quickly thinking of any excuse. How could I manage it? Even my better judgment advised against it, but I hate to disappoint others. It's a double-edged gift/flaw I possess—one that has gotten me into numerous difficult situations over the years. Ask my wife. I often want to be a nice guy—but only with an expiration date. I thought, even hoped, that this gig would be temporary. In a few weeks, they would find someone else to take my place and I'd be off the hook. I never expected that reluctant, superficial pledge would last more than 20 years!

Stepping into this private world, a second floor room in a priest's home, wasn't a huge stretch for me. In my younger years, I had contemplated becoming a priest and briefly took a stab at seminarian life. So being in close quarters with a priest never intimidated me. It was the distance, the unapproachable air I breathed in his presence that irked me. The probability of us developing a friendship seemed remote. For years the only thing we had in common was his disabled body. He owned it. I dressed it.

My testimony to this lack of friendship rests on an awkwardness I felt around Bill for years. I sensed a cold aloofness from Bill that was palpable at times. Yet I seemed to be alone in that opinion. Everyone else seemed to rave about him, describing him in glowing terms such as "remarkable" or "amazing." Initially, and for the many years that followed, I never shared that perspective. Certainly, he was polite enough, but even so, I experienced a thick wall around him.

Admittedly some of my feelings stemmed from my own neuroses, but it was also clear to me that Bill wasn't looking for friends; he was looking for volunteers. I would tell myself,

"Just do the job, and shut up."

Looking back, I'm not sure what I was thinking. Why was I so sensitive? Why did I need or want this man's approval? It might have been the mythic status others gave him. As a result, during that first year of attending to Bill, aside from strained politeness, we maintained almost complete silence with each other.

Some time later, I had the opportunity to purge these feelings and re-place them with new understanding. For many years, however, I felt dis-connected going through this weekly ritual. But I kept it to myself. I would begin the morning by walking into his room with a happy-go-lucky step which was always forced due to long nights walking a crying infant. Within minutes of my arrival, I'd clash with an irritated, helpless quadriplegic. As soon as I'd start to feel uncomfortable, I would open at full force, my compassionate, empathetic valve. And the harder I tried to be friendly and light-hearted, the more I seemed to irritate him. The wall of silence grew thicker. No matter what face I put forward, Bill gave me the impression that I bothered him. It never occurred to me that it was my ineptitude as a caregiver that caused him to be so impatient with me.

After a while, I stopped trying so hard and settled on a quiet, reserved self, only occasionally and insecurely stammering out something regret-tably stupid to fill the void. I hate silences. However, my alternative to them is even worse. Foot-stuffed-in-mouth has followed me through life like a faithful puppy. With Bill, I could do it on command. Because of our lack of conversation, I would confide to my wife that I felt Bill just didn't like me. In her wisdom, however, she would always focus me back to Bill's reality. She would chide me with,

"Why would you expect him to be glad to see you?"

"Because, I'm cheery, and it's early in the morning and I had to give up sleep, and by golly, I'm volunteering!" I'd respond.

"You're dressing him. That's all. And who would be thrilled about being dependent on someone like you?" she'd ask astutely.

She was right.

Eighteen years passed. I kept showing up, kept dressing, kept feeding, and Bill—well, he just kept polite silence, only commenting occasionally on the one thing we did have in common—how much we both hated cold winters. Ironically, on one of these very cold winter mornings, our relationship began to thaw.

I had just accompanied Bill the one block walk from his residence to the high school where he taught Theology. Holding the school door open for him, he motored up the ramp. I then took off his woolen poncho and hat and adjusted his matted hair. Usually after this action, Bill would quietly say,

"I'll see you next time."

Repeating the same sentiment back to him, I would go on my way. This day, however, as I removed the hat, he shyly looked up at me and said,

"If you want, I'm watching a basketball game on ESPN tonight...if you want, I mean if you're not doing anything and you want some company to watch the game, I'm gonna be there...in the monastery...I've got beer."

Laughing out loud, I replied,

"Hold the phone; wait a cotton pickin' minute. Bill Atkinson is asking me to watch a game—and have a beer?"

He chuckled and smirked his slight signature grin that he'd flash when embarrassed.

"I just thought maybe you weren't doing anything," he responded.

Shocked and excited, I detoured home on my way to work to tell my wife.

"Guess what?" I asked rushing through the door.

"Bill Atkinson asked me over his place to watch a game and have a beer!" I was as excited as if I had won free tickets to the Super Bowl. Better yet, it was like I was invited to a surprise party for the coolest kid in school. From a self-esteem perspective, I had won the lottery.

My wife replied,

"You see, maybe he likes you after all."

Cathy always says I'm one of these off the radar, over-sensitive people. And she's usually right. With Bill, however, I argued for years my intuition was correct. I was sure he didn't like me. But this time? I had an invitation to watch a game with him. It was definitely a breakthrough moment!

Later that evening, despite seven inches of snow, I headed over to Bill's place. No mere "weather event" would stop me. Rain, sleet, tornados? No way. Like the U.S. Mail, I would not be kept from my mission. When I arrived, Bill was sitting by the television and actually seemed pleasantly surprised I had made it.

One of Bill's very favorite things to do was watch Villanova basketball games and he rarely missed one live or on television. From the moment I took off my coat, Bill was uncharacteristically talkative. So much so, I could hardly get a word in. This was never ever the case, and as I drank a few bottles of beer I realized how much I enjoyed the sudden role reversal. All in all, we had a very pleasant time.

After the game ended, and I was putting on my coat to leave, Bill started nervously moving back and forth in his wheelchair. Although I said goodbye and turned to walk out, he stopped me and asked a bizarre question, right out of left field,

"You do a lot of writing, don't you?"

"Huh? Somewhat…a little," I stammered totally perplexed by his inquiry.

With my high school English teacher's low opinion of my talent still echoing in my mind, I downplayed my writing as nothing more than some cheap journal stuff. I explained to him that it was more of a hobby, but something I enjoyed nonetheless.

Bill continued on by asking me if I ever wrote poetry. I was honest and said no.

"But can you tell if a poem is any good?" he asked.

"I guess," I replied somewhat warily. "Good poetry to me leaves with an insight."

Bill seemed to need something from me, but I knew I wasn't the judge, critic, or teacher he was looking for and I admitted it. I didn't want to oversell my abilities.

"I wrote a poem," he finally admitted sheepishly. "I'd appreciate if you would read it. It's over on the end table in an envelope with your name on it."

"Really, my name is on the envelope? What's this, premeditated?"

Probably embarrassing him even more I continued,

"You thought this out? Even choreographed the asking by leaving the poem in an envelope with my name on it? First, you invite me to watch a game and now you want to share a poem?"

This was a unique moment for both of us. An extremely private guy asking a low-esteemed neurotic to read his private thoughts? It was enough to give a cynic a coronary!

"I'd be honored," I said, stuffing the envelope in my pocket.

"You will read it, won't you?" he asked hesitantly, "And you will tell me if it's any good? Seriously I want to know."

Yes, I promised to do both and left.

Later that evening at home, I unfolded the paper, and read what would be the first of several poems he would share with me. Here is the poem exactly as he gave it to me that evening:

"FALLING"

Night is falling
Anxieties are calling
I stare into the dark abyss

The night abounds
I hear my breathing sounds
But I know there is something amiss

I had my say
For strength I prayed
To help me through another night

Conflict I'm in
Alone, can I win?
My chances, I realize, are slight

The doubts are near
I sense my fear
The darkness envelopes me more

I fight back the night
With all of my might
But things remain as they were before

Awake I stay
To greet a new day
I realize I must pray again

This burden's too tough
Too harsh to touch
Lord, share this burden and send me a friend

And the blackness remained
Little sleep came
For a friend, I anticipated

She was always there
With words of care
The blackness slowly dissipated

Her words, her tone
I was not alone
The darkness held my heart no more

My doubts she allayed
My fears kept at bay
Sleep came and darkness was not the same as before

Demons still there
Burden is shared
I feel her touch, warmth, and kindness

Sleep is slight
I wake in the night
But, now my mind is not captive in darkness

I have to let go
The process is slow
I must surrender my anxieties of the night

Sleep I try
Anxieties aside
I have time to pray again

She is kind
Has settled my mind
Thank you Lord, I believe we are friends.

The next week, after the initial shock of Bill's sudden overture passed, we spent some time discussing his poem. I explained to him that for my taste, a good poem works on several levels. First, it must use language to give expression to the deep things inside all of us. Then, after reading the poem, I like when I'm moved emotionally, when I feel what the writer is feeling. Lastly, I like when the poet reveals the universal vulnerability in all of us. For me, Bill had scored high marks in all three areas and I told him so.

Clearly, my reaction pleased him. I still can't figure out why my opinion mattered to him. It was one of the rare times in my life that it did. Also, I communicated to him how much it meant to me that he trusted me enough to share it. In his self-deprecating style, he just shrugged his shoulders and said,

"Thanks for reading it."

I took the poetry sharing as a slight crack in the armor. He allowed me ever so slightly into his private self so I took it as a sign and decided to push further. The next time I saw him, I asked him over breakfast,

"Do you think you have any more poetry in you?"

He said he wasn't sure, so I just let loose on him with a Knute Rockne type pep talk, even chiding him in a smart aleck manner,

"Write a bunch of them; you have no excuse not to…you're in a wheelchair…it's not like you don't have time because you're playing too much golf."

He chuckled, thought a moment, and said he would try. And he did— for awhile.

Unfortunately, in June of that year, Bill became extremely ill with another in a constant string of infections. Infections are regular visitors to the immobile. This one episode was serious as Bill slipped into a coma from sepsis. That entire summer Bill fought through another attempt on his life. Death's door was not new geography for Bill, but for years he always mustered the strength to fight back. Using one of his nine lives, he could always keep death at arms' length, but this time it was different. He was seriously diminished, and unable to come out of his corner swinging any more.

No longer able to breathe on his own, his doctor tethered Bill to a ventilator. September came, but going back to teach high school was unrealistic. Nurses were now employed, twenty-four hours a day, seven days a week. The Provincial of his Order decided it was prudent to move Bill to the priests' nursing facility on the Villanova University campus. For the first time in his priestly life he would leave his beloved residence and place of employment, Monsignor Bonner High School.

The move meant that the dressing part of our relationship was over. After twenty years, my short-term, turned long-term, temporary commitment came to an end. Confined to a hospital bed in a strange place, Bill would now have to recover and adjust to an entirely new way of life. The small amount of freedom he had previously enjoyed disappeared.

After week one, he was depressed, angry, and somewhat scared. The one thing he most enjoyed was his interaction with his students and now he would have to pass days and weeks, maybe months, confined to his room, lying on his back. He was proud of the job he did as a high school teacher and he had no plans to retire. He fully expected to return to full capacity and teach again.

Since I also work at Villanova University, I could still visit him regularly. Our first conversation found Bill hopeful that this move was only a temporary state of affairs. Despite the reality that he was very sick, his desire to return to teaching and his old room gave him reason to hope. I soon discovered from other sources that this new home was permanent. This wasn't rehabilitation; it was retirement. Full-time nursing care was his new station. The doctors' assessment confirmed his unlikely return to strength and past function.

Soon after, Bill's sister, Joan, contacted me. At the University, one of my jobs is acting as an advisor to students with disabilities. Hearing my role at the school, Joan felt that maybe Bill could come to my office occasionally and volunteer. From her visits, she could sense that Bill's new idleness was a large pill for him to swallow. She thought that in a few weeks when he gained some strength, he might be able to work part-time in my office counseling disabled students. She reasoned that Bill's working with college students would provide a much needed outlet for him.

"Was there anything he could do in your office?" she asked me one day.

I agreed that if Bill did recover somewhat, it might benefit him and the students to spend some time in my office. At the very least it would give Bill some motivation to get up in the mornings. I assured Joan that if Bill's health improved I would put him to work. Unfortunately, it soon became apparent to all, including Bill, that he wasn't going to recover. The days where he could sit up and move about in an office or a classroom setting were over.

From this point on, my visits with Bill became more regular. He was genuinely glad to have company. He was now much more comfortable talking with me about his feelings. I began to visit almost daily. Stopping in during my lunch hour became routine. Truthfully, not having to get up at 6 A.M. to dress him made me a more energetic visitor. Now that we had reached a comfortable social banter, I genuinely looked forward to visiting. Bill, however, admitted to me that he was having a difficult time adjusting to this new situation. I wished I could do something for him.

One fine late September morning as I walked across campus to his room, it finally came to me—poetry!!! That would be his new job! He would once again have activity and purpose. I would get Bill to write a book of his poetry! Give him an anchor of hope, something active to jump start him out of his new found melancholy. I'm no psychologist and I'm not sure if I understand what constitutes real depression, but I was sure that Bill was depressed. So in my mind, I imagined Bill writing a book of religious or spiritual inspiration. My primary motivation was to get his mind active and off his present woes. Constructing a solid vision for a book, we would take Bill's poems, followed by a reflection on each one and why he wrote it. We would turn this book into something worthwhile to read. Maybe even a meditation for the reader to contemplate. We'd kill two birds with one stone! Get his mind on something new. And, maybe get him to write some interesting poetry.

From this point on, I felt an urgency to act. I sensed Bill was not going to be alive much longer. And so, as I entered his room that day, I made my first pitch to him. He greeted my enthusiastic overture with dead silence.

"Nah, I'm not good enough to write a book."

He was emphatic. No way! He wanted no part of my genius. I replied that plenty of bad books are written all the time so in the worst case we'd just be adding to the pile. In the best case scenario, however, we would be creating a legacy. Once again, he flat out replied,

"No!"

Even though I knew he was extremely shy, quiet, and tight lipped, his reservations still angered me. Here I was concerned with his well-being, trying to fill up a lot of his idle hours and he flat out dismissed the idea. I cranked up one more offer. With forced enthusiasm, I promised him at the very least his family would read it and they would have a piece of him for all time. This tactic struck a chord. His eyes lit up.

"Wouldn't they be surprised if I wrote a book?" he thought out loud.

I egged him on further by telling him that it wouldn't be fair to die and not leave a record of something of himself behind for the rest of us. Finally, he agreed to think about it. I knew I had him. In fact, I knew it was now a sure thing.

The following is the first official conversation we had a few weeks after Bill agreed to attempt a book. In it, you may notice his reluctance. He could be a stubborn man, and I had to hurdle in order to get the project moving. I was peddling faster than Lance Armstrong on a Pyrenees bike path. When I arrived with a tape recorder, he immediately became uneasy.

12th August, 2005

SM: "THANKS FOR AGREEING TO DO, OR, AT LEAST TRYING TO DO IT."

BA: *"I didn't fully agree yet; I'm still not sure. I said I'd think about it."*

SM: "WE'LL JUST SEE HOW IT GOES, OKAY? IF YOU THINK IT'S WORTHWHILE, WE'LL CONTINUE; IF NOT, WE'LL STOP. AND YOU'VE GOT THE RIGHT OF FIRST REFUSAL. ANYTHING THAT YOU DON'T LIKE OR WANT, I SCRATCH.'

BA: *"What's with the tape recorder? You're going to tape this? You didn't tell me that."*

SM: "WHAT ELSE DO YOU SUGGEST? IT'S AN INTERVIEW. I'M THE INTERVIEWER. AN INTERVIEWER HAS TO HAVE A TAPE RECORDER."

BA: *"Can't you just write a few things down?"*

SM: "NO. I CAN'T UNDERSTAND MY OWN WRITING. IT WOULD LOOK LIKE A PRESCRIPTION PAD!"

BA: *"Okay. But you'll tape over this? I don't want any tapes laying around. I might say something I don't like. And you might want to use it against me."*

SM: "NEXT WEEK, AFTER I TRANSCRIBE IT, I'LL TAPE OVER IT. PROMISE. HOW'S THAT?"

BA: *"Alright."*

SM: "HERE'S WHAT I'M THINKING. SORT OF WHAT I CALL A ST. JUDE SHOP BOOK. YOU WRITE A POEM. WE TALK ABOUT THE POEM, WHY YOU WROTE IT? WHAT WERE YOU FEELING? WHAT DO YOU WANT THE READER TO GET OUT OF IT OR FEEL. MAYBE A LITTLE REFLECTION, A LITTLE SERMON OR SOME KIND OF A THEME. SOMETHING LIKE THAT.

BA: *"I only have a few poems and I'm not even sure they're any good."*

SM: "BUT YOU HAVE MORE IN YOU, RIGHT?"

BA: *"I don't know, yeah, maybe, probably".*

SM: "YOU DO, TRUST ME! THINK OF IT AS YOUR GREATEST HITS. HOW MANY SER-MONS HAVE YOU GIVEN IN YOUR LIFETIME?

BA: *"A lot.*

SM: "EXACTLY! AND SOME HAVE BEEN GREAT! SOME HAVE BEEN SNOOZERS. PICK OUT THE BEST STUFF YOU HAVE. IT'S THAT SIMPLE! IF WE HAVE MATERIAL FOR A BOOK WE'LL KNOW AND IF WE DON'T, AT LEAST I'VE GOT SOME OF YOUR THOUGHTS DOWN ON PAPER. AFTER THIRTY SOME YEARS IN A WHEEL-CHAIR BEING A PRIEST, YOU'VE GOT SOMETHING TO SAY! OR YOU'VE GOT THOUGHTS THAT I WANT TO GET OUT. NOT TO BE MORBID,BUT IT WOULD BE NICE TO HAVE SOMETHING BESIDES JUST A FEW NICE SNAPSHOTS."

BA: *"Alright, you're convincing me."*

SM: "I THOUGHT A GOOD START WOULD BE TO GIVE YOU SOME TRIGGER WORDS. I FIGURE, JUST FROM KNOWING YOU THAT SHOWING UP JUST ASKING QUES-TIONS WOULD BE LIKE PULLING TEETH. SO I PUT ALL THESE WORDS DOWN ON PAPER THAT MIGHT HELP US GET SOME POETRY WRITTEN AND ALSO GET YOU TALKING AND OPENING UP."

BA: *"Like?"*

SM: "BIG SHIT...DEATH, FAITH, FRIENDSHIP, LONELINESS, HUMILITY, PERSE-VERANCE, THE MEANING OF LIFE, TRIALS, PRAYER. IS THERE A GOD? THE WHOLE GAMUT OF HUMAN EXISTENCE? THINGS I WOULD DISCUSS WITH A PRIEST. AFTER ALL, YOU ARE A PRIEST, SO MOST PEOPLE ASSUME YOU HAVE AT LEAST A LITTLE MORE INSIGHT THAN THE REST OF US. AND, YOU'RE A QUAD, SO YOU'VE GOT THE IDEAS AND THE EXPERIENCE OF HAVING YOUR BELIEFS TESTED. GOOD SHIT."

BA: *"Is that going in the book?"*

SM: "SURE. A LITTLE PROFANITY WILL HELP SALES."

BA: *"Not at the St. Jude Shop."*

SM: "ALRIGHT SO NEXT TIME, WE'RE GOING TO BEGIN BY TALKING ABOUT YOUR ACCIDENT. I NEVER REALLY HEARD THE WHOLE STORY FROM THE HORSE'S MOUTH."

BA: *"Okay. See you next time."*

After this session I went right home and played the tape. Immediately I realized I had done most of the talking. Bill did seem to enjoy the interview, but he was still reluctant. Being the eternal optimist, though, I was off to the races. We could, at the very least, have some good conversations that would help him pass the time during his convalescence. Breaking through would prove to be a whole other matter. Getting Bill to open up and share his private thoughts would turn out to be a slow, glacial process. He wasn't a talker and I was. Not a great omen. But as far as I was concerned, the ice had cracked. I crossed a significant milestone just getting Bill to agree to begin the conversation. There were still teeth to pull, but I was now energized.

CHAPTER 2

BASIC TRAINING

ONE WEEK AFTER I PITCHED THE IDEA TO BILL, I SAT DOWN TO SKETCH OUT A blueprint for a book of Bill's self-reflection. I listed numerous questions I had always wanted to ask Bill, plus a host of other topics. Our conversations started off painfully slow. A new self-consciousness set in between us. Eventually, though, we started hitting somewhat of a rhythm where Bill began to relax. The regular meetings improved our comfort level with one another. Eventually, I would prep Bill with an idea for the following session. He actually began to show some mild excitement for the project.

Unfortunately, our efforts would get sidetracked early and often by Bill's frequent health issues. When it became obvious that we would never fulfill our original game plan, I believe Bill became disappointed. Even though he finally instructed me to finish the project myself, I had my doubts. My original plan required offering Bill thought provoking ideas and then recording his responses. Without a protagonist I was sunk.

A short time later, Bill died. My passion for this project quickly subsided as well. I had his poems and the transcripts of our conversations, but it didn't seem enough. How could I put this all together in a way that was worthy of such a person? I learned many moons ago that a good idea without good execution is a bad idea. But as I mentioned earlier, Bill's spirit continued to encourage me. I suddenly realized that in addition to the poems and notes, I also had my memories of Bill—wonderful, vivid memories— which I would intertwine with Bill's own words to create a tapestry depicting this remarkable person. And so, having finally decided to finish this book alone, I thought the best place to start was at the beginning of our relationship.

From the very first day, Bill put me through disability boot camp. Like a good soldier, though, it was what I had to go through in order to understand this complex man. As a fresh recruit I was an incompetent and utterly useless aide to a disabled person. I was green and knew little about spinal cord injury.

The memory of that first day is still clear in my mind. Arriving at 6:15 A.M., I found the door to Bill's residence locked. I rang the bell and waited for several minutes. Finally an older priest opened the door. I identified myself as a new volunteer, there to help Father Bill Atkinson. After exchanging pleasantries, he led me to Bill's room on the second floor. Upon entering, I immediately saw Bill lying on his side, strapped into his hospital bed. He knew in advance that I was coming and when I entered we exchanged a polite "Good morning."

Except for a Motown tune playing quietly in the background, an eerie silence permeated the room. I stood for several moments tapping my foot to "My Girl" waiting for Bill to say something. While the Temptations crooned on about having "sunshine on a cloudy day," I grew more uncomfortable. No instructions were given. No casual chatting. Nothing. Just silence. Those few moments seemed eternal. Hesitantly, I finally asked,

"You want me to do anything?"

"Nope, just wait." Bill simply replied, "Wait for Rich."

Of all the people I've met in my life, Rich Heron is the epitome, the gold standard of friendship. A humble, saintly creature, Rich was a constant fixture in Bill's life from the time of his accident to the time of his death. I haven't checked the requirements for sainthood lately, but when it comes to selflessness, loyalty, and dedication, Rich's light casts a long, long shadow. He began with Bill years ago when they were fellow seminarians. Rich eventually left the seminary, became a nurse, then returned to faithfully serve Bill almost every single day until Bill died. On this first morning with Bill, however, I only knew how glad I was that Rich had finally arrived in Bill's room. I was anxious to get started. At least the activity would relieve the uneasy silence I was feeling with Bill.

As a quadriplegic, Bill was completely paralyzed from the neck down, which meant he couldn't move or feel sensation. From age nineteen on, the only moving part he possessed was a head sitting on top of a stiff, lifeless body. Rich asked me to help move Bill across the bed somewhat so that he could pull out the soiled linen. What immediately grabbed my attention was Bill's dead weight. Just moving him a few inches to change sheets or put on a pair of underpants required serious exertion on everyone's part. For the first time ever in my life, I intimately observed the effects of paralysis.

Encountering Bill's total lack of movement intrigued me. The scope of the injury was huge. In a flash, I became acutely aware of my own sense of freedom and ease of mobility. After leaving that first morning I began imagining the sensation of paralysis, even trying to experience the sensation of dead weight. Can't be done. For the rest of the day the thought of my own paralysis stayed with me, though, and I catalogued in my mind all the things I did that required movement. As I took this quick inventory, it dawned on me that I knew nothing about the situation I found myself in. It wasn't as though I had been completely unaware or insensitive to disabled persons. I had some experience working with disabled children in a special education facility for several summers in college. But this situation, up close and personal, smacked me in the face. I had no comprehension of the complexity of a spinal cord injury. My sparse knowledge was about to take a quantum leap.

The very first thing I noticed was that Bill could not scratch himself. Anywhere. As I stood there Bill asked me to scratch his head with a scalp comb. I picked up a round massaging comb in my palm and placed it behind Bill's head. Like a flea infested dog, Bill moved his head back and forth on the comb for a long five minutes. At the conclusion of the scratching, Bill's scalp bled onto his pillow. Rich explained that Bill had psoriasis and that he'd been waiting patiently all night for someone to come along and relieve the itch.

"He loves that," Rich said as if talking about a retriever. Bill's scalp oozed red. Rich handed me a bottle of some type of liquid medicine and instructed me to work the solution into the back of Bill's scalp. As I applied the lotion, Bill moved his head from side to side. He grimaced from the burning of the medicine. At that moment I wanted to ask Bill why he waited all night if his scalp itched so badly. Why couldn't he just call a fellow priest into the room to scratch it? But on that first day, it seemed prudently best to keep my mouth shut. My first job was merely to scratch—and scratch hard—for a long time while Rich simultaneously irrigated Bill's catheter.

Catheter! The second light bulb flashed in my head. Cather..as in catheter, inserted into penis. "Duh," I said to myself, suddenly realizing that his injured brain couldn't tell his bladder what to do anymore. Rich sensed my low DIQ (disability intelligence quotient) and responded with kind patience, explaining quickly that this critical routine was key to preventing urinary tract infections. Rich's light-hearted, easy-going manner relaxed my uptightness. He possessed a terrific sense of humor, but still instructed me in quiet tones what serious signs to look for when monitoring Bill's care.

The scope of Bill's injury, and any spinal cord injury for that matter, is overwhelming. Obviously he couldn't walk, but I wasn't prepared for the chain of complications that occur when the body's electrical system sustains major trauma. Putting clothes on his body seemed secondary to the big problems. Bladder and sphincter muscles are rendered useless, making monitoring fluid output and waste elimination crucial duties. As Bill lay naked on the bed with Rich working on him, my mind wandered while my eyes stared at Bill's groin. Bill sensed my gawking, and then Rich quickly told me to empty Bill's gallon jug of urine which collected throughout the night.

Rich taught me on the first day the steps involved in cleaning Bill's urinary tract. He stressed the importance of sterilizing any and all equipment used in the process. Suddenly I was in the middle of nurse's training. In a short two-hour period I was quickly immersed into the complex tasks at hand. I comprehended quickly the steps I needed to learn, but still I could not begin to grasp what it was like to lay in a bed, completely helpless. The gap between my working body and Bill's disabled one hit me like a sledge hammer. We continued with the rest of the dressing routine.

After the bodily clean-up, Rich and I placed a special type of girdle tightly around Bill's body to hold in his internal organs. Again, with paralysis and loss of muscle tone, none of the body's normal responses can be taken for granted. We put on the rest of his clothing and then lifted his 195 lb. body into an electric wheelchair. Quadriplegics have no balance. In order to prevent him from falling, Bill had to be strapped securely against the chair back. He was then ready to move downstairs where someone would feed him breakfast. We moved to an elevator and descended to the dining room in silence.

As a first timer, I was a bit shell shocked. Later, I would come to know in detail, the social and psychological consequences of spinal cord injury, but on that first day, I left Bill's residence with failing grades. My basic knowledge was thin but more importantly, my empathy shallow. Driving home I asked myself why did the experience flabbergast me?

"You see people in wheelchairs all the time, don't you?" I reassured myself. But up-close and personal is intensely different. As a perfect stranger, it was an odd feeling to travel deeply into Bill's personal space. Though I thought I was making the extra effort to comprehend what it was like for him, I was profoundly naïve and completely preoccupied with my own inadequacy.

To digress a moment here to add further context: There are approximately 11,000 people who injure their spinal cord each year in the United States. The injury mainly affects young persons aged 16-30, and in large percentage, males. Less than half of these injuries are a result of car accidents, with the remainder divided between falls or acts of violence (gunshot or knife injuries). The magnitude of personal suffering as a result of such an injury became apparent to me within minutes of being in Bill's presence. A hoard of questions immediately surfaced in me. What if that were me? Would I want to live in his condition? Could I cope?

From that day forward the questions just kept coming. Yet, I was afraid to ask anything that might appear personal, out of bounds. Being raised to be overly polite, I clung to the notion that one doesn't ask any question that would make someone uncomfortable. In my family, we were instructed never to ask a personal question, particularly if someone were in a wheelchair. I think that's common or certainly was common of people in my generation. I can't remember too many disabled kids living in my neighborhood, but it would have been considered the height of bad manners to ask someone,

"What happened to you?"

As a result, I didn't dare solicit information from Bill.

Unfortunately, keeping quiet led to my frequently making wrong assumptions. I imagined that Bill would not want to rehash old news or painful explanations to a snoop like me. Again, thinking for Bill, I assumed it would be unpleasant to relive the experience over and over while someone stood by gawking. One thing I did sense correctly, however, was Bill's discomfort with strangers dressing him. Particularly in this locale, it was a secretive world. It was an honored fraternity to which I was being initiated. Actually, few people were invited into Bill's dressing circle so I quickly went with the flow and kept my curiosity underground.

Many years later Bill chuckled when I confessed my early fears of offending him. He told me that most disabled people want to talk about their disability. He especially liked it when young children approached him and asked questions as to why he used a wheelchair. Bill felt that answering sincere, honest questions was the best way to clear up misconceptions about the disabled.

"Now you tell me," I answered with exasperation. But at the outset, this was not information available to me so I moved in the hushed tones of Bill's room, curious with questions, but always silently polite.

The weekly routine became a habit. Months turned into years and politeness became the constant between us. Bill did grow comfortable with my presence, or maybe he just didn't have much of a choice when it came to volunteers. I was slightly better than no one. Nevertheless, I followed my father's imperative to "mind your business," and let go of any nosiness. Tough for me, though; I'm hard-wired nosy!

As time went on, I accumulated new questions, filing them away for the day when I would be able to ask them. Most of them involved how Bill managed his condition physically and psychologically day-to-day. The longer I was around Bill, the questions deepened from the physical aspects of the injury to the psychological and spiritual dimensions of it. Why does something like this happen? And why does it happen to a good person? And why, on top of everything else, to a priest?

Bill's situation and others like it have always challenged my faith in the notion of a just, merciful God. How can a kind, loving God, if indeed he does exist, let someone suffer like this? And for Bill, I needed to know how he could continue to believe and have faith in God after such a tragedy? And I'm not talking here about itty bitty "I go to Church on Sunday to keep me out of hell" faith. Bill had this immense, gargantuan, McDonald's "super-sized" faith. As I learned more about his condition, I got more frustrated with God, blaming him for putting Bill through all this suffering.

Typically driving home or to work in my car after a morning with Bill, I'd give God a piece of my mind:

"Why God, do you let this really good person suffer but then let the cruel, selfish schmucks of the world off the hook?" Who's driving this bus anyway? And who's deciding who gets to ride first class and who gets thrown under? You're not doing a very good job, and frankly I'm not too impressed with your overall plan. Maybe you could give me a sign or something to help me understand?   Please?"

I wanted to purge these feelings with Bill, but he was a priest and I hadn't the nerve. I dare not share any thoughts with Bill. What would he think of me? The last guy I wanted to share my agnostic tendencies with was a disabled priest! Years later, however, I finally got my chance. Winning Bill's approval for the book idea, I needed interview topics. All of the questions I had been afraid to ask became my starting point. You might think someone like myself, bursting with burning angst, would start the first interview with some real depth-probing gems, but ironically, my opener was the most basic question of all.

"How did your accident happen?"

In all these years, I had never gotten the official version from the horse's mouth, so that's where we started. Bill gave me the complete story on my birthday, November 10, 2005.

Bill's First Interview: 10th November, 2005

Q: I'VE WATCHED YOU FOR YEARS WONDERING HOW DO YOU DO IT—MEANING DAY-BY-DAY, OVER THE LONG HAUL? BUT TODAY I LITERALLY WOULD LIKE TO KNOW HOW YOU DID IT, THE ACCIDENT, I MEAN?

A: *"I was on the front of a toboggan, and we hit a tree. Nothing exceptional. I don't remember much. I lay on the ground and my first response to my friend Ted Glessner was, "I don't feel too good." Ted found some humor in the moment and I remember him saying, "Let me get you unwrapped from this tree." The rest I don't remember because I blacked out. I know they carried me up a hill, loaded me in a station wagon and took me to St. Francis Hospital in Poughkeepsie. Initially they didn't know how serious it was. One of the priests stationed at the seminary, Father Tony Tomasulo, was screaming, 'I've got someone seriously injured here!'*

"At first, I was just another person in line at the emergency room, but finally someone came out and said something like,

"This person looks like he's seriously injured.

"To which, by this time, this very excited priest shouted,

'That's what I've been trying to tell you.'

"I heard most of this later for I had slipped into a coma. And a coma is a coma; you don't take notes. So I was in the hospital for six weeks in Poughkeepsie and eventually I came out of the coma."

Q: WHAT WAS INITIAL REACTION TO YOUR CONDITION?

A: "Truthfully, I was too sick to care. My breathing was bad; I had a tracheotomy and was on a ventilator. But at this stage, I was probably in denial. I was not thinking about paralysis. It was only after I was transferred to Magee Rehabilitation Hospital in Philadelphia that I finally realized, 'I'm not walking out of here.'

"In fact I still remember there was a physical therapist, I forget his name, but he spent a few minutes explaining how the spinal cord works, and I think I responded, 'Doesn't seem like I'm walking again.' "

Q: NO DOUBT A STUPID QUESTION, BUT ONE I NEED TO ASK: WHAT DO YOU SAY TO YOURSELF AFTER THAT MOMENT, "I'M NOT WALKING AGAIN"? AND YOU'RE A PRIEST, SO DON'T GIVE ME THE PARTY LINE.

A: "I'm sure at first I said, "Why me?" And even though it does sound like the party line, I eventually said, "Thy will be done." I mean, not that day but over a long process. And why not me? I was lucky because I wasn't alone too much. I was surrounded by family and friends and I had lots of constant support. Maybe if I didn't have all the people around me, I would have wallowed in bitterness but *when you lay there, you have lots of time to talk with God."*

Q: YOU WERE A YOUNG KID. ONLY NINETEEN. DID YOU HAVE COUNSELING? THERE HAD TO BE A TON OF STUFF ON YOUR MIND ABOUT YOUR FUTURE.

A: *"I did go to one counseling session. Kind of a funny story. They had a group session and I'm not one for talking, but I thought, "Okay I'll go to the group." We're sitting there and in walks the therapist. His first line to the group, mind you, he WALKS in and says, 'I know what you're going through.'*

    " 'Buddy, you don't know a thing,' I thought, and then wheeled right out, followed by some others in the group and I never had any more counseling."

Q: IS THERE A BOND AMONG THOSE WITH SPINAL CORD INJURY?

A: *"At least to the point that he or she knows the drill. All the complications. All the routine things you once did, now you now have to rely on others.*

Q: YOU WERE IN THE FIRST YEAR OF THE SEMINARY AT THE TIME OF THE ACCIDENT. DID YOU HAVE A DECISION TO MAKE WHETHER OR NOT TO CONTINUE?

A: *"No, it wasn't a big decision, just a logistical thing. The Master of the Professed, Father Keffer, came to me and asked if I wanted to continue and I said yes. Then the training began."*

Q: AND YOU JUST WENT BACK TO COLLEGE?

A: *"Back to Villanova University, with lots of help, I started back."*

Q: DID YOU GET SPECIAL FAVORS OR ACCOMMODATIONS?

A: *"None. In fact in those days all the professors played by the book. They treated me like everyone else."*

Q: AND THE REST IS HISTORY. YOU WERE ORDAINED A PRIEST, WORKED AS A HIGH SCHOOL TEACHER, BECAME A FOLK HERO.

A: *"If you say so."*

We had broken the ice!!! I was no Morley Safer or Mike Wallace, but for my first interview it was okay. To my surprise, the tight-lipped Bill liked talking about himself. And I relished listening. Ah, to be able to probe the mind of a saint. And I did see it as an opportunity to do just that. I would hurry back in a few days with more questions. After hearing about the accident, I wanted to know as much as I could about his initial adjustment to the injury. He had talked about the physical rehabilitation, but I wondered about overall reaction to the injury. I imagined how angry I would be if the same fate visited me. I asked Bill if he would mind if I probed a bit about anger and acceptance. I assumed that these were stages he knew something about and I thought it important ground to cover.

Second Interview 12th November, 2005

Q: I WAS THINKING FOR THE PAST SEVERAL DAYS ABOUT YOUR ACCIDENT. I WAS TRYING TO IMAGINE SLIDING DOWN A HILL ONE MINUTE AND THE NEXT HAVING MY LIFE TOTALLY CHANGE. KNOWING MYSELF, I CAN ONLY CONCLUDE THAT I WOULD NEVER BE ABLE TO OVERCOME THE ANGER AFTER SUCH AN ACCIDENT. CAN WE TALK ABOUT THAT?

A: *"If you want."*

Q: WELL THE OTHER DAY, I SORT OF HEARD ABOUT THE ACTUAL EVENT, BUT AFTER THINKING ABOUT IT, WHAT INTERESTS ME THE MOST IS HOW YOU DEALT WITH...RESENTMENT? WEREN'T YOU SCREAMING AT GOD? OF COURSE, I'VE NEVER SEEN YOU ACTIVELY GET ANGRY SO MAYBE YOU DON'T DO ANGER?

A: *"Of course, I get angry. But I can't remember specifically how angry I was. I was sad, though. But, like I said, I had so many people around me, so much support."*

Q: BUT WHAT ABOUT OTHER PEOPLE WHO HAVE TRAGIC THINGS HAPPEN, UNFAIR THINGS? WHAT WOULD YOU ADVISE THEM ABOUT ANGER?

A: *"I would say anger is part of being human. We have it; we have to learn to handle it or it will handle us. You can't just say, don't get angry or not deal with it because the more you hide it, it'll hurt you in other ways."*

Q: I THINK WHEN I WAS A KID EVERYONE WAS TAUGHT TO SUPPRESS THEIR ANGER. IT WAS WRONG TO SHOW ANGER. I'VE ALWAYS HAD A LOT OF PROBLEMS DEALING WITH MY OWN ANGER. I TRY NOT SHOWING IT. THEN IT USUALLY ESCALATES INTO SOMETHING BIGGER AND COMES OUT AT THE WRONG PERSON AT THE WRONG TIME, AND THEN I FEEL WORSE.

A: *"That's exactly what can happen. I spoke with some people close to me about how I felt. But the truth is—anger could have consumed me. And then where would I be? You have to come to terms with whatever it is that is making you angry. And you have to admit that you have it and are hurting. And I just didn't see how I could survive if I let it take over me. Depression was not something I was going to let happen."*

Q: SO IT WAS AN ACT OF WILL THAT MADE YOU COPE?

A: *"I think, too, that in my situation, I wasn't just angry, I was probably fearful of the unknown. What was going to happen? But I guess I was lucky. I was blessed to have the ability to cope.*

Q: SO THE LESSON IS—ACKNOWLEDGE THAT ANGER IS OKAY, LET IT COME OUT, AND THEN TRY AND MOVE ON?

A: *"If that's the lesson you want, take it."*

Q: ALRIGHT. THAT'S ONE. IT'S OKAY FOR ME TO BE ANGRY SOMETIMES AS LONG AS I DON'T HOLD ONTO IT TOO LONG?

A: *"You can hold on to it as long as you want, but if you want to move on, you better let it go at some point. I learned that how you talk to yourself about things affects how you deal with life. If you keep telling yourself it's hopeless then for sure it will be hopeless. I chose not to go that way."*

Q: THAT'S A GOOD FINISH FOR TODAY AND MAYBE WE'LL COME BACK TO THAT.

CHAPTER 3

THE STRENGTH OF OTHERS

I CAN THINK OF NO WORSE EXPERIENCE FOR AN INDIVIDUAL THAN A SPINAL CORD injury. To comprehend living without physical sensation or movement is unfathomable. Add to the paralysis, the long list of health problems that follow the injury. It takes a powerful imagination—one I don't possess—to grasp the scope of the injury. Sadly, no one but the injured can. Watching Bill day in and day out was as close as I ever wanted to get.

The remarkable thing about being witness to Bill's life was the absence of any complaining. Ever. Zero! Nada! Not once in all of the years I was with him did he ever whine, "Poor me." Sometimes I wish he had, because as I watched, I would continuously mutter, "Poor you!" If he had complained once in awhile, it would have made him appear more human to me, less Jesus Christ Superstar. If he had screamed out my own internalized anger about the unfairness of his situation, I would have broken into applause. But that, of course, never happened. In fact, the one constant in all my years with Bill was his remarkable patience with his own suffering. It was not surprising then that Bill often compared himself and his disabled condition to Job from the Old Testament. He once contrasted his own trials to Job's saying,

"Job might want to take a page out of my book."

Despite this enormous acceptance of his condition, for many years it remained disturbing for me to be so close to Bill's daily struggles. I'd often leave after a visit and then experience melancholy for the rest of a day. Trying to comprehend why he received such a large share of pain always bothered me. I had yet to ever hear a satisfying explanation as to why bad things happen to good people. Bad things happening to bad people troubled me, too. Job, or Bill, or anyone else—it made no difference

One day for the hell of it, I asked Bill if I could ride around a bit in his motorized chair. He was in bed so he said,

"Go ahead, if you want."

I rode around in the chair for several minutes. I had seen this done once as a sensitivity exercise in a disability awareness program. In hindsight, though, it was a very insensitive thing to do since the wheelchair was his own personal mobility. It was also very stupid of me. After several minutes riding around, I was able to stand up and walk away. End of comparison. I was stuck with only a superficial spectator's point of view. It would take a lot more sensitivity on my part if I were to ever traverse a path to more heightened awareness.

Interviewing Bill years later offered me the opportunity to take a few more steps on that path. It helped me to understand his situation better, and how he coped with it day by day. One of the first things we talked about was Bill's situation relative to others with the same injury. He considered his path atypical of most spinal cord injured patients. He explained,

"Relatively speaking, I was privileged."

He further recounted,

"I had a great support system with my family and friends, and there was money to take care of me. After all, I am a priest and I'm part of a religious community. Few people have that luxury. Most people in my situation aren't that fortunate."

Privileged? Fortunate? Had I heard him correctly? Had he really used those words to describe himself? I was totally at a loss to understand how he could feel this way about his own suffering. As a result, when I finally became comfortable talking with Bill, I began expressing my anger and confusion about what I perceived as senseless suffering. The combination of his strong quiet presence as a priest, and his seemingly saint-like handling of this incredible burden, made me think I might get some reliable answers to life's mysteries, especially on this subject.

Like so many people around Bill, I had adapted this universal perception that he was a person who seemed to have life all figured out. Perhaps he would be the person who would finally help me make sense out of suffering. Of course I had already accepted the fact that suffering was part of the human condition, but the many responses or explanations for it I heard throughout the years never set right with me.

"We can't understand the ways of the Lord," was the typical response I heard a lot growing up. Sure, blame it on the Lord. The whole idea of waiting it out and taking it on the chin for a greater reward in the afterlife frustrated me.

In the beginning, Bill patiently would echo this same annoying tactic,

"We have to accept things as God's will."

His advice on this subject, like with most things, was for me to learn to let go of my anger. He would often remind me of the prayer,

Grant me the serenity to accept the things I cannot change.

Despite countless attempts at doing so, I continued to ask,

"Why God, do you allow so much human suffering?"

Bill and I would converse often about God and his motives or at least my perceptions about His motives. I was getting to a point with Bill that I felt just comfortable enough to share several private thoughts without fear of his judgment. A few conversations into our now regular interview sessions, we discussed our one-sided God dialogues. Bill stunned me one day when he admitted that he did have many doubts about God:

"Probably more than most," he confessed. "Sitting in a wheelchair, one thing you have is plenty of time. I have a running argument with

God about his plan for me."

I asked him to explain to me as best he could how he really believed his accident fit into God's plan?

"And what about all the suffering he piled on? Is it God? Is it random?" I asked. "Tell me Bill, please, does God work like the *Wizard of Oz?* Is he controlling the dials behind the curtain, or are we floating out here aimlessly on our own after the big bang accident?"

Whenever I would ask these types of questions, Bill would always look at me with a "Whaddya want from me?" kind of expression. But I would press on. One day I finally posed the most obvious questions—the ones most people thought of when they met Bill.

"How do you find the will to face your life day in and day out? Admit it—you got the cosmic screw job! And what if it's all for naught? What if there is no heaven? What if you just had one unlucky moment?"

Bill quietly absorbed my barrage. He quickly became used to my stream of consciousness habit of letting thoughts fly unfiltered. Nothing fazed him though.

Continuing my tirade, I remarked,

"I know you told me that you're not depressed, but you have to be— all the time. At least I think you should be! You know, you have a right!"

What I really craved from Bill at this moment was his strength, and I admitted it to him,

"I covet your super-human ability to take life on the chin. I can't. I don't take suffering well. Head cold, sore throat? I'm bitching to God or the life force or whoever or whatever is steering this boat we're on. Just answer me one thing. How you can still believe in this God"

You'd think I would take time to breathe between existential quandaries, but it felt good finally asking Bill these questions. It had been a long arduous journey with Bill since our days of no conversation. I felt like a man dying of thirst with an oasis finally in sight.

Bill paused a long moment. I thought to myself,

"Wow, I stumped him."

He lay there and said nothing for a long, long moment. For a second, I thought maybe I had angered him. Finally, he answered my list of why's with a very simple, unemotional,

"Why not?"

Nothing else.

"That's it? That's what you've come up with after all this time?" I yelped.

"Yeah." was his short reply.

With the tenacity of a pit bull I refused to drop this subject. So, in subsequent interviews I would keep coming back to all of these whys and hows. One day, tired of listening to my constant tirades, he expanded on his original answer and finally gave me a response that helped me understand what the whole thing was about.

> *"Tragic things happen all the time, don't they? What makes me different than anyone else?" he explained. "Pick up the paper this morning. Blame God if you want. Go ahead if you must. That seems easy to me. All I can tell you is this—at 6 A.M. this morning, God sent me a huge cross to crush me. That much I'm sure. But at 6:01, he sent a lot of people to help me carry it."*

Without any hands to hold a hammer, Bill had succeeded lovingly, but most definitely, in banging me over the head with one.

I finally came to realize that his style was to deflect attention or admiration away from himself by giving recognition and praise to others. Paying homage to the goodness of family and friends, Bill's position was that God carefully and deliberately sent regiments of reinforcements to help him cope with his daily battles. It was not surprising then when Bill eventually got to his second poem it was a tribute to his family and friends who had made all the difference in his life.

"THE STRENGTH OF OTHERS"

"How'd you do it?" people would say
So confining, day after day
Having others around for constant care
Ever wonder if life's unfair?

"How'd you do it?" people would ask
Is it better now than in the past?
To see others do what you did before
Realizing you can't do them anymore?

"How'd you do it?" people have said
Needing help in-n-out of bed
Doubts at times? Patience wearing thin?
Ever wonder how it will end?

"How'd you do it?" day after day
This path taken wasn't my way
The choice was Another's, not my own
He sent me help. Couldn't do it alone.

How'd I do it? Let me confide
Always with others right at my side
Family and friends from the start
Gave me love in no small part.

How'd I do it? Day after day?
Would not have it, any other way
They shared triumphs and setbacks too
Been blest when I look in review.

How'd I do it? Let me reply
On those who help me, I totally relied
They taught me to live, not just to cope
With their love they gave me hope.

How'd I do it? Day after day?
Help of others along the way;
Valued friends, sisters and brothers.
I simply borrowed—the strength of others.

Bill was very pleased with this particular poetic effort and remarked,

"I wrote this because I got tired of people inquiring all the time, 'How do you do it?'

"Like I did?" I asked.

"Yep, just like that. So now you know; I put it in a poem."

Aside from enlightening me, this poem also provided a bridge to subsequent discussions on friendship and family. As our interviews progressed, Bill led me through the stages of his adjustment to his injury and how he felt blessed to have his family and friends around him at all times. Many spinal cord injury patients labor in a depressed state, experiencing feelings of anger, hopelessness, or worthlessness. Bill gave his family most of the credit for his strength and capacity to move on with his life after the injury.

"At first, I think your mind reacts as if nothing happened, as if it's just something temporary, but like I said, I knew early on I wasn't walking again. But others around me, and in patients I've met since, yes, there's a stage of denial or that's the clinical term doctors would use."

Immediately I followed with the big depression questions,

"Were you depressed? Are you? How often did you want to commit suicide?"

"Depressed?" Bill asked. "How do you define depressed?" He explained that he experienced a "deep sadness which still comes once in awhile but it's not as frequent as when I was younger. You do sort of play your old life over and over again for some time. But I wasn't depressed in a way that I would have to be medicated or need to seek out psychiatric treatment. I was probably worse than I admitted, but I don't remember all the particulars since I was so sick for so long. But after it settled in, I guess I had a choice."

In his semi-sarcastic manner he then asked me to answer my own question:

"Do you think you would be happy after breaking your neck?" He did, however, assure me, "But I never contemplated suicide. I'm sure I was angry, but I was lucky to have the parents and my brothers and sisters who rallied around me," he continued, speaking fondly of the Atkinson clan.

"There were always people around me, always concern. Certainly my family first and then I had so much caring and help from my fellow Augustinians and so many friends."

Bill's praise of his family launched my own reflections as a parent and sibling. The impact of this injury on family members could easily be overlooked. Certainly family members don't experience loss of feeling or movement, but, in a way, they are experiencing the death of the loved one as they knew him or her. The extent of physical suffering is limited to the patient but gets exacerbated exponentially when we consider parents and siblings. Family members grieve for their loved one; they have feelings of sadness and a new life is thrust upon them filled with fear and uncertainty. How will their lives be impacted?

The new financial reality of having a dependent person can also be overwhelming, and as Bill pointed out several times, the financial burden aspect is more of the norm for many spinal cord patients. The cost of supporting a disabled person is extremely high, and round the clock medical care becomes crucial. The stress on families can be crippling, leading to questions and sacrifices that no one ever expects to face. Roles and priorities within the family change. For parents, dreams they had for their child are shattered. These dreams are replaced by anxieties such as, "What happens to my child when I'm gone?" Small, commonplace parental worries about family routine no longer matter. Permanent care moves to the forefront and along with it, the accompanying demands and costs.

Bill repeated to me on several occasions that it was strictly his family's rock solid foundation that gave him the motivation to continue. He lived with them and through them. He confided to me that he had inherited his internal toughness and quiet guard from his father. Because his father had been strict with him, Bill felt he had the courage to face anything life threw his way. When questioned as to how his accident affected his parents, Bill would explain,

"Pop didn't say much immediately. He was a tough guy who handled things as they came up. Mom stayed in New York the whole time. For all of the recovery. She didn't leave my side. She and Pop took care of me during home visits. We didn't discuss much about it. It happened and everyone just pitched in and helped me."

Reminiscing on his childhood, before his accident occurred, Bill further recounted,

"I was blessed with great parents and that's one thing I've continually appreciated over my years teaching— not everyone gets great parents. And my mother was a strong person. Kind, generous. Belonged to every church group possible. She had to be something because my aunt used to say, 'You'll never know how much she changed your dad.' Dad was a fighter, a real fighter. Got arrested for union activities. Assault and battery with intent to kill. So he had a temper. Got tossed out of school. Mom softened him. He never cursed around the house. We were scared but around my mother, he was quiet. I knew my father better than my mother. She died at an early age and I was away from home. Teenage years I'm in my own world. But she was a family person, emphasizing family, cousins, aunts, uncles. Like I said, big on church activities. She didn't react to the priesthood. At my deaconate, she was dying of cancer but I think she was happy about the whole thing."

"My childhood was great. We got everything we needed but there was no excess. My father was strict; my mother the easygoing one. I do remember the dreaded words, 'Wait 'til your father gets home.' I would rather be punished always by mom. Dad was the enforcer."

"Did you get hit back then?" I asked.

"Some. Never in the face. Always on the rump. I think there's still room for some hitting on the rump. Parents today have seemed to abandon that tactic altogether, but it was effective on me. But baseball was my dad's sport and he took us to the park and taught us baseball. To give Mom free time. Good memories. Good. Wrestling, I remember. Meeting him on the way home from work. Racing him home. More of those memories than anything else."

When Bill's Dad died at age 91, Bill was sad but wanted very much to talk about his father. I only met Mr. Atkinson on a few occasions but I knew they spent a lot of time together. Father and son would spend summers together at their beach house. Bill reminisced,

"In his older years, Pop and I spent a lot of time together. He would often say, 'I don't know how you did it everyday.' But, you know, he had to endure it too. But he kept a stiff lip. Pop was a man of a few words. Very few. When I announced I was going in the seminary, he put his hand on my shoulder and said, 'Whatever you decide, your mother and I are right behind you.' Always encouraging."

Throughout his life, Bill maintained an undying loyalty to his father. Later, as his father aged, the tables turned somewhat and Bill felt satisfied that he was able to look after his Dad in his old age. I would occasionally visit the two of them at their beach home and Mr. Atkinson, like his son, was a man of even fewer words. But I sensed a closeness that both men felt deeply, but men being men, they usually sat in silence. I think caring for an aging parent gave Bill the feeling that he was able to "pay back" somewhat for the parental love he received.

A few days after his father's death, I asked Bill if there was anything he needed. The ever pragmatic Bill replied,

"My Dad was a great family man and a loyal friend; there's nothing else that needs to be said. He's with God and my mother so I'm sure he's happy."

He spoke with great confidence saying,

> *That's the reward for a life well lived, when that person leaves you feeling privileged for having known them."*

After sharing with me his thoughts about his accident, his family, and his childhood, I finally began to feel comfortable enough to broach other personal subjects, so I suggested for our next session that Bill share some of his great insights on the topic of friendship.

"Give me a sermon on what it means to be a true friend," I requested.

He agreed that he would like to give it some thought and said that he had some definite thoughts on friendship that he'd be glad to share. I came back within the week and recorded a conversation about friendship. I began our next visit on a personal note,

"I guess now that I'm helping you with this book, I'm in. I'm a friend, right?"

Wryly he replied, "Don't rush it."

I wanted his sermon, his lesson learned about friendship. "The Strength of Others" pays homage to all of those friends but I wanted to go a bit further.

"Define friend for me," I requested.

"I don't have the ability or words to crystallize friendship," he responded. "I just know I couldn't get through life, particularly this life I've got, without friends. My friends (and my family are my friends too) are my foundation."

I told Bill I always like the quote from *Ecclesiastes* that states, "A faithful friend is a strong defense and he that hath found such one hath found a treasure."

But Bill preferred Jimmy Stewart in *It's a Wonderful Life,* or I think it was Clarence the angel who said,

"Remember no man is a failure who has friends."

I then topped him with one of my very favorites from *The Wizard of Oz*:

"How about what he says to the Tin Man? 'Remember my friend that a man is not measured by how much he loves, but by how much he is loved by others.'"

Bill agreed but then pointed out, "But Dorothy didn't want to leave the Scarecrow once he got his brains so I guess it's good to have friends with brains."

True.

"Why are you a good friend?"

"I'm not sure," Bill stumbled, "You'd have to ask others. But what I really try to do is listen. One thing I've learned over my years as a priest or teacher is that the thing that people need the most is someone to listen to them. Someone to just give them time when they need it. That's hard to do. And it's one of the few things I can do. I think the most important gift you can give to someone who is your friend is your attention. Just silent attention to someone who needs an ear can heal someone's pain. I think listening to someone's confession is that act of true listening with understanding, and no judgment. That's a gift that not all of us can give. And

it's something we have to learn to do. I always love when I meet someone who just sits down and wants to listen to me."

Bill was one of the greatest listeners I had ever known and I paid him that compliment. He blushed and then joked,

"I'm sort of stuck listening, aren't I? I can't just walk away. And if I get really bored, it's looks bad if I motor away."

But over the years what I noticed about Bill most was that he could sit and patiently listen and not get rammy like I often do. That was impressive to me. Not that it's a big confession coming from me, but I have a hard time sitting still and being present in the moment. When I confessed this to Bill he instructed me in the essence of friendship,

"I'm lucky to have some really good friends who do it for me. Sometimes I just like sitting with a friend. I don't have to talk. You have to talk."

Maybe I was getting the essence of the drift between our two continents. I talk non-stop and he can sit in silence. He could sit for long periods in absolute silence. I can't stand silence!

"But I can!" he yelled in response.

"And it makes me nervous," I defended.

"Silence sometimes is good. Just spending time with someone. I don't need to do a lot of talking. Sorry."

That cleared things up somewhat and I understood that it wasn't all me.

Another issue, I wanted to get at was dependence on the kindness of strangers.

"Doesn't that bother you?"

"It would if I thought people were being nice to me because they felt sorry for me or they felt I was a duty or a chore. But I've been on the receiving end of a lot of kindness from many people. I can tell you people are good. And I've received kindness and love from friends and family so if there is a silver lining in my injury, that could be it. Speaking of friendship, I always liked C.S. Lewis. Found him to really speak to me. He said that friendship is that moment when one person says to another, 'What! You, too? Thought I was the only.' "

I think that's a nice way to explain friendship."

So that day I learned that good listening and non-judgment were keys to being a good friend.

"What else, Bill?"

"I told you, everything I have, I got from someone else. IF I was going to write a sermon, I'd start with someone else's material and work my way into it. Someone like Henri Nouwen. He wrote that a real friend is with us when we're confused, when we despair, when we grieve; a friend is someone who can tolerate not knowing or curing or having answers for us. I like when people are with me in my suffering. That's what I've experienced from a lot of people. The reality is: I'm powerless and I need friends to help me get by."

Now I had something else to shoot for. I always have this tendency to listen and then follow with advice but Bill warned me,

"That's sort of a point I'd make. Most people know the answer if they talk out their problem out loud. A good friend just aids the process of self-reflection."

I felt pretty good that day.

"Thanks!" I said as I turned off my tape recorder.

❧

Several days later after Bill and I had this little talk on friendship, he dug out a letter for me to read. The next time I came to visit he asked me to read it. The letter was to his friend, Cathy, who lost her husband. It wasn't a poem but he was very proud of this letter. He said he felt that this particular letter served as a symbol of how he tries to be a friend. I think he was most proud that the text he wrote was a clear representation of himself and the type of honesty I wanted for his book. The letter which I reprint here sums up nicely Bill's concept of friendship.

Dear Cathy,

I am sorry to hear about the death of Kevin and I am also sorry that I could not be there to celebrate his mass of Christian burial. Be assured of my prayers for Kevin, you, and the entire family.

I also write to narrate a dream that happened to me last weekend. As you well know, there are no limits on space and time or human condition in a dream. Most dreams cannot be remembered the following morning, but this dream was so striking—let me just tell it as I remember it.

There we were. Just two men walking down the beach. It was Kevin and I talking about events in the past. I was carrying some books. Although I do not know the reason I was carrying them. I found this odd because Kevin and I never had any lengthy discussions. Afraid that this dream would end quickly, I asked him, if he could say anything to his family, what would it be? He started to talk and the words were so moving that I looked inside one of my books for a piece of paper. I had one piece of paper but no writing instrument. I turned to Kevin and asked him,

"Do you have a pen?"

He reached into his pocket and pulled out a pen and gave it to me. I began to write down most of what he said for I had forgotten some of his narration. When he finished, I gave him back his pen with heartfelt thanks. I had the feeling that my dream was ending, but he was going farther along the beach. There was a part of me who wanted to follow him, because I knew the separation between us would be painful. I also realized that if I did not let him go, he would never reach the end of his journey.

When I woke up the next day the dream was still vivid in my memory. Of course it was only a dream. There was no beach, there were no books, but strangely enough there was a piece of paper on my bed side table in a hand writing I had long forgotten. I pass this paper along to you with the intention that you may find some solace, hope, and joy.

Love,

Bill Atkinson

After reading the letter, I remarked to Bill that I was sure that Cathy, whoever she was, must have experienced a deep comfort from reading it. Bill said that was his only hope.

"It was only a small thing I could do."

Bill's letter to Cathy epitomized his deep caring for others in need. One big theme he always spoke to me about was the importance of paying attention to small things because we seldom get the chance to do the big things we want. It would be grand to have money and power to help the millions in need but Bill, like Mother Theresa before him, sought quietly to do everyday acts of mercy or extend the simple hand of friendship to everyone he met. His last line to me on friendship was,

"I can't touch or feel someone's hand but I can touch and feel their heart."

Slowly, yet most definitely, my "why do bad things happen to good people" thesis was being picked apart. Bill had taught me that friendship was part of the universal genius of creation. He explained,

"I have faith because friends have helped me learn faith."

I was now convinced the role and importance friends have in helping overcome tragedy and sorrow. As a result, I wanted to keep going with the theme of friendship and the role his relationships had in his recovery. I needed to hear a good priest dispensing good advice. But whenever I came to a conversation using the direct mode Bill would pull back saying,

"You're putting me on a spot here. I don't consider myself an expert."

But he couldn't convince me after all the years and countless people who confided their most intimate feelings that he hadn't picked up a thing or two.

"Isn't that sort of a mainstay of priesthood, helping people with their relationships?" I prodded.

"That's true," he said, "I have listened to a lot of people and that's been a part of priesthood and you're right that people expect a priest to have answers."

"But you must know something just from being in the occupation," I continued annoyingly. Patiently, he explained,

> *I know that I have experienced a lot of love from family and friends and I'm lucky. And I try to bring love to all of my relationships.*

That response, however, was too generic for me. I needed something a little deeper.

> *You asked what I thought and I think this is how God works through us. Through our love of others. Relationships are chances to bring God's love to others. It's not always easy but if you approach all of your relationships as a chance to know God or let God work through you, then I think we can improve our lives. Without love, where would I be?*

> "COMMITMENT. BEING PRESENT WITH SOMEONE WHILE THEY'RE STRUGGLING WITH PAIN. THAT'S THE GIFT WE CAN BRING TO OTHERS. IS THAT IT?" I QUESTIONED HIM.

> *I think that's what we're called to be. If anything is going to make*

sense, it has to come from what we bring to a relationship. Many people ask me how they can fix their lives. They're unhappy and they want me to give them a quick answer. Whether it be a divorce or just a problem with a sibling, they want to blame something and then want me to agree. I guess I try and tell people that you can't fix someone else. If there is a problem in a relationship, I find a good place to begin is with myself, asking if I'm the problem. Look in the mirror. I think Father Don Burt has the best analogy. I once heard him preach that we're all broken clay pots. God makes everyone broken in some way but gives us love as a way to mend the brokenness. I always believed that the toughest thing about Christianity was to love someone who was difficult to love. And sometimes I'm that person who's difficult to love. IF we acknowledge that we're just as broken as the other guy, then we can try and be more understanding of the imperfection of others."

On the rebound I said,

"You know, there are some people I just can't do that with. There are just some people that I struggle to find the good in. Help me with that and I'll leave you alone for the rest of the day."

"I didn't say it was easy," he confessed, "And to be honest, I'm not saying you have to get along with everyone. Sometimes you have to walk away. But you asked for my advice on relationships and my advice is to try to find God in others, even if you do end up walking away. Bring love to others—no matter what your excuse—is a good way for me to put it."

"So love God by loving your neighbor even if your neighbor is a jerk?" I proudly asked, like a young student eager to share the correct answer.

"Unless your neighbor may be thinking you're the jerk."

The strength of others was a great lesson!

CHAPTER 4

LEMONS AND LEMONADE

ONE OF THE MOST INSIGHTFUL QUOTES I EVER HEARD CAME FROM DR. EARL Bader's Dramatic Literature course at Villanova University. Dr. Bader once made a statement in that class that has stayed with me for all of my adult life, and whenever I run into him, after all these years, I remind him of that fact. Of course, he modestly gives credit to someone else for the actual quote but his words echo daily in my mind:

"Life is about how you deal with your second choice not your first."

No matter where I look, I can find no statement, no quote that more aptly applied to Bill Atkinson.

At eighteen, Bill Atkinson made a choice to enter the seminary. He was young and strong. One year later he suffered a major spinal cord injury that left him paralyzed for life. In the blink of an eye, his life had changed dramatically. While no one in their right mind would choose to live as a quadriplegic, the fact remains that thousands of people do so every day. The difference among them is HOW they choose to live with this disability. Bill was a shining example of someone who made the most of his second choice. And those who knew him and learned from him are decidedly the better off for that fact.

During our initial interviews, when I was still trying to crack the ice with Bill, I opened a conversation by asking him,

"WHAT WAS IT THAT YOU WANTED TO BE WHEN YOU GREW UP?"

His response was muffled with a few "Ums" and:

"I don't specifically remember," but he did recall one point during his senior year in high school when he decided to study for the priesthood. He ascribed his seminal priestly leanings to his observations that the priests who had taught him in high school seemed to very happy people. He elaborated on his decision process by explaining,

> *"The priests I came in contact with just seemed to me to enjoy what they did, and I watched them carefully, then decided, I think I'll give that a try."*

Harking back on my own experience, I tried to imagine making a life decision of such magnitude at eighteen. In fact, it was unsettling to me when my friends and peers could make such life commitments after leaving high school. I was still having trouble making a shopping list! In fact, in those days I believed that an individual, such as Bill, who could make such a huge decision about the rest of his life, must have had access to some inside information.

The nuns and priests I knew always spoke of having a "calling" as if God had personally tapped them on the shoulder. Were they, as many Catholics described, individually called by God to the priesthood? And what was that calling all about? I was curious. For many Irish-Catholic families at that time, having a son or daughter enter religious life meant the family had a direct line to heaven. With a priest or nun in tow, a family's stock in the Catholic community definitely rose. Later, of course, many nuns and priests exited the Church as if there were a fire, and those ideas vanished with the exodus. As a result, I wondered if Bill had ever regretted making his priestly decision at such a young age and with little to no life experience. Since he left for the seminary right after high school, I wanted to ask if he ever thought he made a mistake.

"DID YOU EVER WONDER HOW DIFFERENT YOUR LIFE WOULD HAVE BEEN HAD YOU NOT GONE INTO THE PRIESTHOOD?"

Surprisingly, he confessed,

> *"I've played that scenario out many times in my head…Sitting for*

most of my life, I've thought of everything," he mused. "Lots of times I've asked what my life would have been like if, let's say, I decided to go to college or get a job instead of the seminary," he directly responded.

Did he regret making such a decision at a young age without the benefit of experiencing anything beyond his small parochial world? I zoomed in with my Earl Bader question, asking him about his first and second choices. Bill perked up instantly and assured me that his priesthood was not a second choice for him.

"My decision to enter the seminary was easy, but to stay was the more difficult choice," he acknowledged, "and today I can look at you and honestly say, I made a conscious decision to be a priest."

He further explained that his disabled condition "was a second choice if you want to call it that–or perhaps no choice at all. But you do make a good point about life is about all the other choices but your first."

Continuing on this topic, he reminisced,

"At nineteen, your health, your future, your thoughts about what's coming next—no one plans on an accident. That's why they call them accidents…All of a sudden you're on your back or in a chair for good. Think about that again—I was nineteen years old when the accident occurred. At first, I thought I might just lay around forever, dependent, and that scared me."

Bill skillfully and clearly took me back to the depth of that experience. As he went further into the details, I began to understand why he was so businesslike with his caregivers.

"You lose your freedom," he said almost tearing up.

With no freedom, his ability to make individual choices was severely compromised because he was forced, to a certain extent, to live at the complete mercy of others. Bill admitted that his loss of independence was the hardest thing he had to accept, explaining,

"To this day, I am conscious and still work to take control of my circumstances. I get upset when I can't take care of my own needs and that can really make me angry," he stated almost seeming to know what I was thinking.

It was the admission I needed to hear. Yes, he gets angry, he admits it. One admission cleared up a lot of misconceptions on my part.

At this point, a bolt of guilt struck me as I thought about all my years with Bill. It was the first time he actually admitted to me that he feared being dependent on others from the very beginning of his rehab. Never once had I realized that Bill's negative feelings I sensed toward me were really tied to this issue of dependence. I suddenly became very quiet, allowing the real crux of Bill's disability to penetrate me deeply. Bill waited on me for a second to follow up with another question. The anger, self-pity, resentment that I would personally feel and display if I were in his place became palpable, real. I sat in silence for a moment. Bill asked,

"Are you okay?"

"Yeah, I'm sort of just thinking of that whole dependence on others idea…you know I'm sorry but for some reason, I never understood your attitude. I think I'm finally beginning to understand."

Personal decision making and control over his environment was something I had witnessed in Bill and now that I understood I could begin to atone for the many times I wrongly interpreted his shortness or lack of patience with me. Why was I so naïve and surprised by this? Probably because growing up we were taught to place priests high on the pedestal. Years of Catholic upbringing skewed my perception of priests as above the fault line of the rest of us. I had Bill on the perfection pedestal. Because he was so quiet and reserved in his feelings and conversation, I assumed that he accepted everything and should be grateful for my presence. I was one of those kind strangers he depended on and oh, how stupid I was!

Despite his total dependence upon others, however, Bill explained that he made one of his first post-injury goals that he would never let his injury imprison him.

> *"I remember deciding rather quickly that I better, for my own health, decide on what I was going to do," he emphasized. "You can go down pretty fast to the level of self-pity, and I've seen a lot of people do that, but I thought for me the best course of action was to get on with my seminary training and continue what I started."*

I asked how big a deal was it to go back to the seminary?

> *"It wasn't a huge decision for me, mostly just a logistical thing."*

At the time the "Master of Professed," (the head of the seminarians) Father Keffer came to Bill and asked him if he wanted to continue and Bill said that was his desire. And the rest of his training began. He went back to Villanova University to complete his undergraduate degree and then with lots of help, he started classes. In 1965, there was no Americans with Disabilities Act. As a result, there were no special accommodations available to students as there are today. Bill explained,

> *"All the professors played by the book and treated me like everyone else so I guess that was a good thing."*

Looking back on the obstacles Bill faced back then, one could easily consider him a disability pioneer.

> *"There was no disabled culture or societal support like there is today," he admitted, "That an injured person would go back and try to put his or her life together was not an accepted practice. There weren't any opportunities or few that I knew about for quadriplegics. In fact, it was a pretty sure bet that a disabled person would probably end up being institutionalized in a nursing facility."*

Bill admitted that many of his initial post accident fears were centered on the whole notion of being unable to "do anything in the world of employment."

"But I was lucky. I didn't have lots of time to dwell on it. For many people I knew in my situation, institutionalization became the reality. But I had the opportunity to get back on my horse somewhat. But yes, that was a scary time."

Trying to lighten our discussion a little, I joked with Bill that the priesthood was a great option for someone with a spinal cord injury—there was no heavy lifting involved—except for the occasional tortured soul.

"Never thought of it that way," he replied to my twisted logic.

At that point we began discussing, in earnest, the limited options available to spinal cord injured persons finding that second choice. High vertebrate spinal cord injury disrupts not just the body but also a lifetime of dreaming. Interests, daily activities, hobbies, and most of all career aspirations end for many patients. Bill had always been an active sports enthusiast and he told of his genuine sadness about not even being able to toss a baseball or shoot a basketball anymore.

"We all take those things for granted," he cautioned me, "Just a reminder to you when you hit your next golf ball—wink at God and acknowledge the gift."

Gratitude for such small things was Bill's guiding light.

❧

One particular interview that I had with Bill brought out some troubling aspects of disability and the challenges we still face today as a society to assist these patients with meaningful re-entry into society. Even today, with great advances in technology, awareness, and accommodations, the life of a spinal cord injured person is still laden with fears and obstacles. Post-injury Bill had adequate and substantial resources behind him throughout his recovery process. Both his religious community and his family stepped forward with Herculean support, but as Bill himself pointed out,

"What about those not so fortunate who suffer this injury?"

What opportunities exist for those who are disabled to find meaningful employment, especially those who do not have resources or education or family to fall back on? A floodgate of questions came pouring out of me, and I expected Bill to answer every one. He was reluctant to speak with authority, but to me he was extremely knowledgeable about disability laws and rights and in his quiet way, he did play the role of disability advocate. He had a lot of information at his fingertips and he had a handle on the importance of having disabled persons employed in good jobs.

> *"If those people are going to move forward in their lives, they've got to have purpose; let's agree that a good job gives someone purpose," he followed.*

Frequently, we would discuss the ADA and its effect on the disabled community. Later, in my role as a University advisor to disabled students, Bill offered me great insights from the disabled person's perspective. Bill felt that though the ADA had opened some avenues in terms of educational opportunities,

"There really isn't a ton of businesses extending a 'Welcome Disabled Persons' sign."

Bill emphasized the importance of spinal cord injured persons establishing the goal of gainful employment. He reiterated that rehabilitation goals kept one in life's game both psychologically and financially.

Sadly, many studies on this subject reveal very low rates of employment varying between 40% on the low end to 85% on the high. Bill pointed out that nurturing the spirit of the patient is equally or even more important than treating the physical maladies.

> *"I don't think a disabled person is ever happy about being disabled but once that fact is accepted, you go on, and if you have opportunities to continue to contribute, you have hope. I have a working (at least I think it's working) brain, so I believe I can contribute something," he added.*

Bill also made me aware of another aspect of employing disabled persons; that is, despite protective laws, an employer has a set of assumptions the moment he spots a wheelchair. If a person who uses a wheelchair manages to land a job interview, he must deal with the interviewer's pre-assessment and unspoken doubts. Bill told me of many experiences where he was given polite treatment because of his priestly collar and wheelchair, but in reality, he still fought discrimination because of his situation

Fortunately, after completing his seminary training, Bill did have a job. At Msgr. Bonner High School, Bill found his all important purpose and then managed to influence this school community for over 25 years. Admittedly, Bill got lucky because the school and the religious community to which he belonged were willing to accommodate all his needs. Bonner became home because it was structurally accessible and the administration was eager to have Bill on the faculty. Though he had a modified teaching schedule, he threw himself completely into the life and spirit of the school. As a club moderator, sports team cheerleader, or school chaplain, Bill's influence quickly spread, adding to his mythical status over the years.

Since Bill had an extensive teaching career, I thought his educational philosophy and self-evaluation would make a good topic of discussion. One cold, cold January morning, I asked him what makes a good teacher and why was he a good one? Bill smiled and replied,

"Ever notice you ask me questions that are too big to answer?"

"OKAY." I SAID, "LET'S KEEP IT SIMPLE THEN. LOOKING BACK, WERE YOU A GOOD TEACHER OR NOT?"

"I'm not sure I was."

"GIVE YOURSELF A GRADE."

"I think you should ask the students I taught," was his escape from the question.

I told Bill that it was not my intention to chase down hundreds of kids to get a scientifically valid opinion. Bill finally came clean with,

*"I guess I tried to be a good role model and share what I had to offer.
I believe teaching is one of the most important jobs in our society.
It's a cliché, but just think about the people who influenced you and
me the most. Besides family, who are the memorable people in your
life? Most likely, a teacher or a coach, which is sort of the same."*

Teaching was meaningful to him and he confessed that he truly loved
being in a high school environment. Bill's prerequisites for future teachers included:

*"…a passion for the job and a love for kids—that's what makes a
good teacher. Teachers who don't like kids make me scratch my
head."*

"I never disliked walking into school.," he continued. "There are kids
that get under my skin, but I try and keep every student's interest at
heart even when they don't believe it sometimes."

I had heard rumors that Bill could be a "bad-ass" sometimes.

*"Bad ass? I guess I can still intimidate from a seated position. That's
a good thing, don't you think?"*

I questioned him further on this subject. Did he work extra hard on
being a bad-ass to compensate, or to make kids feel he was in total control?

*"I think I would have been that way, wheelchair or standing," he
admitted.*

"What else makes a good teacher, Bill?"

*"I think a teacher, a high school teacher, has to understand
teenagers. The best teaching I did was not in the classroom. It happened in hallways or lunchrooms or gyms. The biggest part of my
career and the thing I took seriously was the fact that students
would come to me with all kinds of issues and they trusted I could
give them some guidance. A teacher has to wear many, many hats.
Teacher, counselor, adjunct parent, police officer."*

Bill believed that as a priest and teacher, students trusted him deeply and let him into their lives. High school students are growing up. They're confused at times, even angry, making wrong decisions, trying on new identities. A teacher had to understand that and go with it.

> *"That was a big part of my success, I guess. I understood the big picture and didn't take my own class and role too seriously. I also think teachers can learn from the kids. If you are flexible and open, you realize that you don't have all the answers and sometimes the students can point out things you need to change. And, humility is a big part of good teaching to me."*

When two teachers get together and talk about education, it's inevitable that the topic turns to dealing with parents, so I asked Bill,

"WERE YOU GOOD WITH THAT ASPECT? PARENTS?"

> *"I'd tell the parents the same rule I used myself. Try and be consistent with your kids. No magic pill. The worst parents I encountered never saw a problem with their child. The best parents were the ones willing to acknowledge that their son or daughter wasn't perfect or that there was a problem and that they were willing to go to any length to solve it. You ever hear, 'Perfect kids come from perfect parents?' There exists neither."*

Bill was always honest about what he didn't know. When we talked of parents he reminded me,

> *"Anything I say about parenting is armchair quarterbacking because I'm not one, remember?"*

"BUT," I ASKED, "HOW ABOUT ADVICE FOR PARENTS AFTER DEALING WITH THEM FOR ALL THESE YEARS?"

Bill believed we could spend a whole book just on the subject of parenting, and reminded me we were straying from our initial idea of writing a book based on his poetry.

> *"I could talk about good parents and bad parents all day long, but*

anything I say is just opinion and since I haven't walked in the shoes of a parent, I don't think I have credibility."

Since we were on the subject of parents, I asked Bill, a veteran schoolteacher, if he had a credible definition on what makes a good parent.

"I was never a parent, so I better be careful. But I had great parents—so here goes my definition: To be a parent is NOT to be a friend. You may become that later on, but you need to have rules and regulations, always tempered with lots of love and affection. And most important. Be consistent. That's what I can say about my parents. What they said, they meant."

At that point I asked if Bill ever thought about his potential as a parent. Did he wonder about that?

"I probably would have been stern with my sons but with daughters I would abdicate over to my wife 'cause I'm old fashioned. Easier for me to probably raise boys. Girls would cry and I'd compromise."

"YOU'RE A SEXIST," I REPLIED.

"I guess, if you say I am," he shot back.

⁓

By now it was very easy to talk with Bill. At the end of each interview, he would anxiously ask me when I would be back. Ever the conscientious teacher, he would even critique my failures as an interviewer and offer suggestions. He would even begin an interview sometimes saying, "Don't you want to know about…?" and then offer a particular topic of interest. After a few months, it was if we had been doing this for years. There was no strain, no effort on either of our parts. And ever the willing student, I was absorbing so much about his world as a priest, teacher, and disabled individual. Most importantly, because his losses had been so great, yet his coping with them even greater, I had learned an important life lesson taken from his own experiences. He explained it this way:

"All of life is about loss. Everyone is losing something all the time.

You're losing time. I think that's the hardest part of being alive, coping with loss everyday. My paralysis is just another one of life's losses. A huge loss. If you're looking for a point or a lesson, I think that we face loss from Day One and we learn that's part of the challenge of living. All of us—we're losing something every minute. People die; we lose our health eventually; we lose jobs. But if you learn acceptance, and that time heals wounds, you can actually get stronger as you go."

Did Bill think that he was stronger because of his experience?

"I only know that grief and pain are just as big a part of me as happiness and joy. There is sadness and loss all around existing side-by-side with new life and new opportunities. It's a cycle. I don't have any great words to describe it, but I can only say that with my pain, with my suffering, people have been with me. Many have come to my side to lift me up both physically and spiritually. And many times, even sitting in a wheelchair, I have been able to do the same for others. There is always loss, but there's also new opportunities always to experience life in a deeper way."

In his quiet, unassuming ways, Bill gave me the answers I had sought after for years. Learning how he dealt with his second choice was one of the most important lessons I took from Bill.

Chapter 5

BIRD'S EYE VIEW

"R EALISTICALLY OR UNREALISTICALLY, DON'T PEOPLE EXPECT TOO MUCH FROM priests?" I asked Bill one day. "People want their priests to be beyond the scope of human imperfection. They get angry or feel disappointed when they find out they're human beings just the same as we are," I protested.

Although Bill agreed with me, he qualified his remarks by adding,

"No matter what goes on in the world, we took vows and we have to be true to them. We should have self-control. We should not fall in love with material things or power or self. I believe my job is to be present. To heal if I can. To touch people in a place where they may be suffering and let them know God's love for them."

That sounded like too tough a job for anyone I knew—especially someone confined to a wheelchair.

"It is a tough job," Bill concurred, "the toughest of all jobs—but a great one, nevertheless."

Ironically, I was soon to witness, first hand, how tough a job the priesthood really was.

One activity Bill and I mutually enjoyed was eating breakfast, especially at a good pancake joint. Perkins Pancake House was only a few blocks away from Bill's residence, and I was always quick to accept an invitation there for blueberry pancakes with blueberry syrup, blueberry butter, and any other type of blueberry they could muster. Every once in awhile, usually on a holiday break from school, Bill would diffidently ask,

Do you think you could drive me down to Perkins?" Bill would never ask directly, "Do you want to join me for breakfast?" or "How about if I take you out to breakfast?" Instead he would deliver a straight forward request to drive him somewhere. In retrospect, I believe the Perkins invitations were his way of showing me a small kindness and saying thanks for coming regularly to help him.

One particular Easter Monday morning, we were both off from school, and on this early spring morning, I was the only person to show up to get him dressed. The entire house was empty except for Bill. Normally, a house cook would be available to prepare breakfast for the priests, but she also had the day off. From the minute I arrived, I could tell Bill was reluctant, even agitated that I alone would have to dress him without any help. Not only was I an inept dresser, but I'm sure he worried even more that I would hurt him while transferring him from his bed to his wheelchair. My amateur caregiver status gave him absolute reason to be anxious. But this day he and I persevered. With his impatient direction, I dressed him, placed him in his chair, and got him down to the dining room.

The only available breakfast foods that day were an odd assortment of cold cereals, which on any given day would have suited Bill just fine. Entering the dining room, however, Bill asked, "Do you have to be anywhere this morning? Would you drive me to get some breakfast?"

Up until then, I had never driven Bill anywhere. Dressing him all alone had been tough enough, but now he wanted me to get him into his specially equipped van. If he had known previously of my utter and complete inability to operate complex machinery, I'm sure he would have taken the cold cereal!

A van with its mechanical lift and a nuclear reactor might as well be one and the same to me. Simply put, I am mechanically challenged, and that's all there is to say. I confessed as much to Bill, but he provided the very specific directions needed to get him securely placed in the van. After carefully following the routine designed to anchor Bill's chair safely in his van, we were on the road. Moments later, we arrived at Perkins and reversed the whole procedure. To my utter amazement, we soon entered the restaurant.

The cordial hostess at Perkins seemed to recognize Bill, but addressed her remarks to me instead,

"Do you want a table with extra room?" she inquired helpfully.

Like so many people do when confronted with a disabled individual in a wheelchair, she spoke exclusively to me—as if Bill were incapable of speaking for himself. And turning up the volume, as if he were deaf as well, she added,

"Does he need silverware?"

Feeling annoyed and frustrated, I wanted to respond sarcastically,

"No, he can just share my fork—or better yet, we'll just use our hands," but wisely I resisted the urge, and politely followed her to our table through a crowd of curious stares.

That's another interesting thing that one learns when traveling with a quadriplegic—people want to look or even stare to such a degree that you can actually sense they're working hard not to appear to be staring. But a quadriplegic dressed like a priest always guaranteed a few gapers.

After being seated, a waitress reminiscent of Flo from the TV sitcom "Alice," brought us menus. The waitress had a weathered look from years of restaurant wars dealing with bitchy customers, thin tips, and slow cooks. Clearly, by the time she got to our table, she had had it with slinging chow that day, and growled,

"Coffee?"

Bill only drank weak tea from a large glass mug through a large glass straw, but I gladly accepted a whole pot. Then Bill surprised me by requesting chocolate milk. Up to this point Flo hadn't noticed Bill's condition. When she finally did look up at Bill, a good looking man with a Roman collar sitting in a wheelchair, Flo's frown turned suddenly upside down. She coyly asked,

"Father…you are a father aren't you…what can I get you, Father… Anything you want you just holler, and I'll get it for you, Father."

After she departed, I suggested to Bill that Flo was sending him a "vibe" and if he decided to give up celibacy, he had a sure taker in Flo.

"She's just your type," I kidded him, but Bill remained all business with her, simply ordering bacon, eggs and pancakes. He was too shy to flirt and my joke had made him even more self-conscious. It still amazed me, though, that wherever we were in public, people magically let down their guard and became available to him.

That is, most people did.

Across the aisle from where we sat, an older man, somewhere in his early 60s stared at us. Think: Wilfred Brimley's twin. Plaid shirt, cranky creased forehead. He gazed toward us over his reading cheaters, taking a break from his morning paper, trying to take in the scene of a priest in a wheelchair. Immediately I sensed the man looking at Bill and I glanced over several times trying to get a quick read on the situation. The man seemed agitated and eager to speak with us.

As we waited for our order, we eased into a conversation about the nice spring weather and how my kids loved Easter egg hunting the day before. Bill was always consistently interested in my family and thank God he was because it often filled in dead conversation space.

When our breakfast finally arrived, I began feeding Bill his fried eggs with ketchup—just the way he liked them. As I mixed up this disgusting tomato egg porridge and slipped it into Bill's mouth, I noticed a woman at an adjacent table feeding her young child as well, getting more food on the floor than in his mouth. I wondered if that weird feeding juxta-position crossed Bill's mind as it had mine, but he was obviously too hungry to observe anything but his breakfast. I, on the other hand, held onto that thought just long enough for Bill to say,

"Yo, another bite, please."

Just a few forkfuls into our meal, I also noticed the man across the aisle continuing to look intently our way. No longer able to keep quiet, and with a belligerent tone, he finally called over to us,

"You a priest?"

Bill politely nodded, and then flashed me a quick side glance signifying,

"Here it comes."

Bill rolled his eyes as the man's voice increased loud enough for the rest of the restaurant to hear.

"What the hell's going on with all these priests screwing all those little boys?" the man bellowed out. "It's a damn disgrace; that's what it is, and you oughta be ashamed of yourselves!"

It must be noted here that on this particular morning the first news stories about the clerical sex scandals were beginning to surface, and it was clear by this man's tone that he had some readied hostility waiting for the next available Catholic representative he met. It was not a great time to be a priest—or even a Catholic for that matter. Many people were conveniently broad-brushing the entire organization as "child molesters," and this particular guy had his guns fully loaded and aimed at Bill. He wanted everyone to know that he was not afraid to confront these sex abusers disguised as holy rollers. We were sitting ducks.

I could sense Bill's discomfort.

But with his brain working overtime trying to figure out how to defuse this verbal time bomb, Bill suddenly transformed his nervousness into a polite smile. He moved the only body part he could by shrugging his shoulders and adding a slight smirk that could non-verbally say,

"Back off!"

By this time, however, several pairs of silent, seemingly judging eyes were fixed on our table and people were either voting with the man or feeling sorry for us. My own self-consciousness over the recent headlines made me believe the vote was about 100 to 0 in favor of the anti-clerics. Like Bill, I tried to smile and finish my breakfast while continuing to feed Bill.

The beast had been released, however, and the man would have no part of granting us even a moment's peace. Louder and louder he continued, ranting,

"What do you have to say about it? Really, I'd like to hear what you have to say about it."

It always fascinates me and admittedly stirs my ire when people don't possess public antennae. This was a man who didn't care the least that he was embarrassing us or disturbing the other diners or most importantly making a fool of himself. He continued with some other observations about the state of morality in the world and demanded that Bill defend his involvement with an organization "that lets queers molest kids."

That did it! I finally made a move to go over to the man and ask him to leave us alone while we ate. Or maybe I was just going to shove a bagel down his throat. Bill quickly shook me off, though, and said with his eyes,

"Don't worry, I've got this covered."

These were the situations Bill had learned to master. Throughout the exchange, he was unflappable, maintaining superhuman composure. He allowed the man to go on and on and on for what seemed to be a hostile eternity. Bill understood that the man had what he wanted, an audience. It was a cathartic bully pulpit. Even the waitresses and hostess stopped pouring coffee to take notice. Flo, who by now had taken a liking to Bill, couldn't even break the cycle by bringing me extra creamers. After a few minutes of being verbally accosted, Bill quietly asked the man,

"Do I look like someone who holds a big position of authority?"

Suddenly the man quieted down.

"I'm just saying that the whole thing is a disgrace; that's all I'm saying, if you know what I mean," the man said softening his tone.

Bill kept a saintly timbre, never lifting his voice beyond a quiet whisper. He had spoken to the man as a loving father trying to calm a hysterical child, reassuring him that he, too, was troubled by the recent news about the scandal and that it was important for us to pray for all of the victims and the abusers. Bill had plugged his finger in the dyke. The aggression pouring from the man immediately ceased. Refusing to grab the bait, Bill had let the situation run its natural course. Reacting with peace instead of anger, Bill had turned the man's rant completely on its head. Like a skilled masseuse, Bill loosened the locked up tension and replaced pent up rage with calm. Moments later, the man returned to reading his paper, realizing he had definitely picked on the wrong guy.

Unlike this man, I now felt like screaming,

"Hey, are you blind, he's a quadriplegic! You got any decency at all?"

To compound my frustration and incredulity, when Flo came to deliver our check, Bill asked her to add the man's breakfast charges to our bill!

Without fanfare, we quietly finished and slipped out of the room and exited to the parking lot. As I pulled out the wheelchair lift from the van, I heard the man's loud booming voice from the doorway shouting,

"Hey, wait a minute!"

He approached the van, saying,

"You didn't have to do that…what's the big idea?"

Bill just smiled and asked,

"Are you feeling better now? You needed to get all of that out. I was glad to be there."

The man, most likely speechless for the first time in his life, stood blabbering for several minutes trying to ask forgiveness in a circuitous fashion—or maybe he was trying to justify his attempt to publicly humiliate Bill.

Though no one in the restaurant heard our farewell conversation, the man now introduced himself as our new friend Bob. He assured us that he realized that not all priests were sex offenders and "though I'm not a Catholic, I know that there's some good ones."

As we prepared to drive away the man asked Bill for his name and assured him that the next time we were eating at Perkins, he would return the favor and pay our check.

 "I don't like to be on the short end, you know, 'cause I like to spend it if you know what I mean," he promised.

Facetiously I took out my appointment book and tried to nail Bob to a date; I was fairly certain that Bob was as cheap as he was loud. I gave him three dates in which we could meet him for breakfast, but he continued to laugh, never actually planning to ever make good on his promise. It didn't matter, though. On this early Easter Monday morning, Bill had achieved a small moral victory. I would have preferred taking some of Bob's money, but Bill was content with making his understated point.

As I drove the van back to Bill's residence, I shook my head and complimented Bill for his kindness and patience with Bob. I was still a little hot under the collar about the whole episode but humbly, Bill gave me added perspective.

"It's no big deal...that's what God calls us to do for one another."

That was all he said. We drove the rest of the way in silence. I lowered Bill on the lift gate, he got out of the van, and I made sure he got back into his house. We swapped mutual thanks for the breakfast and then I added an additional one for the lesson in human kindness. He shrugged it off as just another day at the office.

I reflected on this incident many times in subsequent years, for it served as the perfect metaphor for Bill's priestly purpose. Even with no mobility or strength of limbs, Bill could move mountains with no more than his patient silence. Years later I asked him if he remembered the incident. I joked one day,

"I wonder how old Bob's doing?"

Bill assured me that if we went to Perkins at any time, it was a sure bet that Bill would run into him again,

"And I'd probably get stuck with another check," he chuckled. He then added that the man was just one of many people sent by God to challenge his role as a priest.

"From where I sit, I've got a bird's eye view of life. Since I can't walk or run away, I'm always a captive audience." He confessed that once he put on a Roman collar a neon ad flashed, "I'm waiting to listen to your problems!"

There were two questions that I've asked myself as a Catholic that came out of my recollection of the "Bob" incident. First, it made me think about what IS the role of a priest? And second, what are the characteristics that make up a good priest? After growing up in both the Church and Catholic schools I witnessed priests in all shapes and sizes. The technical requirements of priesthood obviously are centered around administering the sacramental life of the Church and ministering to followers of Jesus Christ. In my home and schools, I was conditioned to place priests and nuns in high regard, deserving or not, always saints never sinners. Clearly, the recent events that plagued the Church had forced all Catholics to admit that deification of religious was naïve at best and more than likely a bad habit that we'll pay for both monetarily and spiritually for a long time.

During future visits with Bill, I never passed up a moment to compliment him on his exemplary priesthood. Bill would always point out to me that he was a priest, an Augustinian, above all other roles, and this was his most sacred commitment. As I became closer to him towards the end of his life, I experienced many, many moments where I felt I was in the presence of an extraordinary, holy man. I learned he was one of those people that you only read about. Why it wasn't apparent to me earlier, I'm not sure. Either Bill kept that side private or my head was thicker than I ever knew. Either way, I now categorically put Bill in the company of great holy men of Church history. Thinking back to the images of saints past, I now conjured a picture of the distant future where people might sit around and talk about the life of Bill Atkinson, as people today reflect on the lives of medieval saints, like St. Francis of Assisi. It's ironic, though, that this reflection usually takes place AFTER the saint has taken his leave of this earth. I'm sure there were even some people who lived and walked with Francis who failed to appreciate his saintliness, only seeing his eccentricity. For all the bad press the Catholic Church has received, though, they can most definitely claim a long line of holy people that stand up to historical scrutiny.

Once I had canonized Bill a saint in my own head, I was determined to get as many of his revelations down on paper as I could. I don't casually throw around the word "holy." I've never been exactly sure what it means outside of reading Webster's definition of "sacred, spiritually pure." It seems subjective to me to judge someone as spiritually pure since you can't see spirit. I've always felt that holiness is one of those qualities that you just know it when you see it. Bill's holiness and getting his definition on priestly character made for more useful conversation topics. One morning, while Bill labored hard to get some oxygen, I asked him what were the qualities that made a good priest? He answered my question with,

"Why not just what makes a good person?"

I was thinking more in line with society's expectations of the clergy. Was it realistic to believe that we could place such high demands on the moral characteristics of fellow humans? Now that priesthood, at least in my circles, was taking a hit from a fan perspective, I asked Bill to give me some self-defense tips.

"I don't think I can help you defend the priesthood," he said. I reminded him of Bob's unfair attack at the pancake house. Bill responded that he could only do or be what he claimed to be, no more, no less. He couldn't be responsible for public perception or for the behavior of other priests.

"THEN LET'S JUST TALK ABOUT YOU AND YOUR ROLE," I SAID. WHAT CHARACTERISTICS MAKE A GOOD PRIEST AND WHAT SHOULD THE REST OF US EXPECT FROM OUR PRIEST?

Again Bill answered a question with a question,

"Did you ever notice that you always want me to give you a definitive answer when one doesn't exist?"

I told him that was a credit to my new found belief in him. This was the cost he was bearing for allowing me into his private thoughts.

"You have to start with the Eucharist and the sacraments because that's the basis of priesthood."

I realized that was the party line response I expected, but I wanted more. I wanted his take on the human stuff that attracts people to the priesthood. What are the tangible things that keep priests in the game, and make them effective through their lives? Like for myself, I expect a priest to be an expert in spiritual life. Really good at it and then be able to help me get better at it.

"And, that's a big part of it," he conceded. "Priests need to continue to evolve in their relationship with Christ, God. But everyone, you too, are called to do the same. Aren't you? So my journey is my journey and yours is yours and you can't put it all on the priest to make you spiritual."

How about inspiring? Didn't Bill think that people want special inspiration from their holy people?

"That's not always easy either," he explained.

I asked him the bottom line,

"WHAT DREW YOU TO IT; WHAT KEEPS YOU HERE?"

"As far as basic things that drew me to it? Desire to do God's work. Giving service to others. Being available to people in their hour of need. And also to share in their good times. Charity towards others is important."

Bill admitted that many, many times he'd have to dig down deep to be charitable. He confessed,

"I don't like everyone I meet, as you know. But I've got to get through some times when I don't want to and that requires God's help. Prayer is very important to me; it's what keeps me in the game.

What kind of praying works for you?

"Easy," he instructed, "God's right here with me and it's on ongoing conversation."

"SO A GOOD PRIEST PRAYS, CONTEMPLATES WHAT THE HELL WE'RE DOING HERE AND THEN RESPONDS BY HELPING PEOPLE FIGURE THAT OUT?"

"That's your one way of putting it. Or I'd say just helping each of us to live a virtuous life, loving one another, respecting our fellow man, and even appreciating God's gifts in someone else."

I walked away from these conversations thinking priesthood is a very tough road. The old Catholic catechism instruction—to love God and love your neighbor—needs priests to move it forward. That is a daunting challenge, day in, day out. We all have days when we're successful at being a good human being, but priests don't have the luxury to let their guard down. High expectations come with the dress code. Bill liked to use the shepherd image to describe himself.

"I like that image and I try to reflect on the life of Christ and imitate his actions, you know, shepherding or tending to a flock; that's a good role for me."

Patience, kindness, love—this was the mantra. Bill jokingly admitted, "That may be an oversimplification, but I can't make it more complicated than that 'cause I'm not that smart."

Yes, others, scholars and theologians could give you a more theologically based explanation of priesthood, but Bill gave a simple, direct explanation of what he did and what he thought others expected of him.

After this lesson on priesthood, I walked back to my office and reflected on my own unreasonable expectations of priests I had known. Bill made me understand that my thought processes on this subject needed some re-evaluation. Once again, in his simple way, Bill taught me the importance of not judging or being too critical or expecting too much from others, when in truth, we're all struggling with the same humanness.

For the rest of that day I thought hard about the idea of basing one's life's work committed to Christ. When faced with the same decision, I flinched. One time long ago, in a seminary, I had a difficult time pledging my life to the historical figure of Jesus. The Christian life appealed to me, but I wasn't keen on a life of celibacy, poverty, and obedience. It seemed too much to ask and I decided they were demands I couldn't live with. But Bill was the best example of what it could and should be. He was true to exactly what he said he was.

Our conversation also got me thinking about the shortage of priests today and how the diminished opinion of religious people hurts society overall. Reflecting on my youth, when my world was full of priests and nuns, it was as if we enjoyed a whole class of designated "holy" people. There was a security in knowing that there were these spiritual signposts, holders of universal wisdom, trying to make me—and my community—better.

Bill Atkinson and committed priests and nuns like him played an important role in helping me bridge the gap between earth and sky. They served as buffers between the unsettling encounter between the known and unknown. Bill simplified the world for me by embodying love, charity, and generosity. That's what I really miss about him. His quick, easy, almost simple-minded clichés about life and "God's plan" for us might have been repetitive but he believed strongly, lived with commitment, and loved unconditionally. In a secular, cynical world that rushes to judge anyone daring to make a commitment to something as remote as "Christ," maybe we ought to reconsider the role of designated holy folks, like Bill.

CHAPTER 6

DOUBTING THOMAS

ONLY A FEW SHORT MONTHS INTO THIS BOOK PROJECT, MY RELATIONSHIP WITH Bill underwent a major transformation. We went from exchanging sparse words with each other out of sheer necessity to suddenly opening up and sharing our innermost thoughts and feelings. I found myself totally relying on Bill for spiritual guidance and counseling. And though he was living moment to moment, breath to breath, he seemed to be comfortable with this new role. For myself, I continued, proceeding as if he would be around for years even though we both sensed his condition was dire. The prospect for a long collaboration was fading fast. But still, I would go home to plan interviews and compose questions for our next meeting.

Initially, I had given Bill a list of trigger words on a sheet of paper that I hoped might stir his creative juices, choosing words like suffering, perseverance, forgiveness, friendship, and faith. Looking back on the experience, I realize these words reflected concepts with which I was wrestling. I wanted Bill to give me magic bullets. I asked Bill,

"Can't you just manufacture some clever things you've dished out already? How about your sermons?"

He insisted that his preaching was mostly spontaneous and contained little planning.

I tried another method, consisting of Bill reflecting on a specific word, getting in touch with his artistic and religious feelings, and then hopefully spinning out some Rumpelstilskin gold. Bill thought this was a good plan and for several weeks, he worked feverishly composing verse after verse.

Unfortunately, I didn't have the heart to tell him that some of his poetry was becoming forced. He was practically reducing complex spiritual ideas to poems like, "Roses are Red, Violets are Blue, God loves you, Whew, Whew, Whew!" But he had enthusiasm, to say the least, which continued for several months as we formed a skeletal outline of what our inspirational tract would become. Unfortunately, our jump out of the gate was stalled when he fell into another serious bout with illness. He became too weak to continue.

As he lay, breathing through a respirator, I would continually encourage him that it would only be a matter of time until we returned to full speed.

"Meanwhile," I instructed one day, "as you lay there, get the poetry muse fired up!"

Even though he initially resisted the whole idea, he felt sad, believing he was letting me down. I would kid him saying,

"If only inspiration had struck me ten years before, we'd be on Oprah's 'Book of the Month' list by now".

Whenever I would visit, I encouraged Bill with the good news that at the very least, we were committing his insight and maybe some poems to paper for posterity. Instinctively, I had always believed that one day the Church would make Bill a saint. And I must admit here and now in the present, that I romanticized my role as the official chronicler of St. Bill of Atkinson's seminal literal work.

One day, when he couldn't speak back because he was too weak, I told him to close his eyes and imagine a hundred years from now. After classical texts like the "Marx-Engels Letters" or "The Diary of Ann Frank," could he see "The Life and Times of Bill Atkinson?" He'd grin with a strained chuckle; I could tell the project finally meant something to him. In fact, during this last year of his life, no matter where Bill and I would begin a conversation, we would immediately go to a place of meaning for both of us. For years, I wanted to know what made him tick. I wanted to know what answers he held to my great questions of God and existence. Wholeheartedly, I was convinced he knew all of the secrets while I had no faith at all. With his next poem, however, Bill confessed to a chink in his armor. Until I read this, it was always me tapping him for answers, but for the first time he expressed out loud,

"I have to find God every day."

"FAITH"
(December 2005)

Sky turns grey
Dawn-a new day
Daylight overcomes the darkness.

In the day
My unrest at bay
I became aware of his closeness.

Shade of the trees
Whisper of a breeze
I feel he almost surrounds me.

Hear him in the din
And the quiet within
I find myself no longer lonely.

To live in the present
To reveal in His presence
Day offers me hope and relief.

But, the shadows will grow long
The day is now gone
Help me in my unbelief.

When he handed me this poem, like his very first effort, Bill was unsure of my reaction.

"Is it any good?"

At this juncture, our relationship tolerated straight communication. He preferred that I'd be direct. He would take my criticism and go back, work the poem, and show me a revision on the following visit. Sharing this poem also gave me permission to probe his newly revealed uncertain self. Our sessions became a mix of confession and values clarification with me playing doubting Thomas. I longed for definitive faith answers from this reluctant mystic.

One beautiful thing about our friendship was that I learned to trust Bill enough that I could be honest about my own feelings about the Church and my ongoing struggles with life and faith. I guess middle age, mid-life crisis, or whatever begins to churn inside oneself, brings a more intense introspection. For me, this introspection produced numerous doubts about the habits and routines of the organized Catholicism where, because of my upbringing, I was deeply entrenched.

Being employed by a Catholic university, and raising my children in the Church obligated me somewhat at least to wear an agreeable Catholic face. However, in recent years I had become increasingly disconnected to all that was drummed into me since childhood. The whole experience was stale. As a parent, I was going through a lot of the motions. For several years, I felt anger and disdain for the whole orthodox lifestyle. When I confessed this to Bill, he actively encouraged me to be critical, if not downright negative.

"Real faith only comes to you when you question," he told me.

He would listen to my rants about the Church, priests, authority, much like he did for our friend Bob from the pancake house. And whenever I get the floor, I like to take advantage. Since I was the product of an extremely strict, dogmatic Catholic father, I carried around some major issues. I also had a Protestant mother (who later converted to

Catholicism to keep the family peace) who sometimes fed my rebellious side with a Reformation mentality.

Up until then, I'd had never admitted to myself that throughout my whole life a quiet religious war was being waged in my head between the good Catholic and the seditious one. For as long as I could remember, religion was a source of conflict in my life and rarely was something that gave me a peaceful, easy feeling. Even in adulthood, at work and in my parish community, I felt a subtle peer pressure from friends and neighbors to go along with everyone else.

Guilt ridden, obedient and eager to please, I put on a good Catholic boy face for the nuns and priests; as an adult, I let the role continue. Altar boy, upstanding citizen, I lived up to the image that I thought my community expected while a latent teenage rebellion seethed inside me. Increasingly discontented, I stopped going to Church and withdrew from any talk or practice of Catholicism. Myopically, I hyper-focused on the hypocrisy of the Church or what now seemed to me a pointless exercise and a waste of my precious time. Given a venue to complain, I enjoyed unloading on Bill. Each visit, he would politely let me go on and he'd carefully allow me to exorcise my demons. One powerful gift he possessed was the knack for sitting, listening, occasionally shaking his head, as if to say,

"I understand."

He would neither agree nor disagree but just quietly listen.

Sometimes, though, that silent response would get to me. Raising my voice one day, I demanded,

> "COME ON; ADMIT IT. DON'T YOU FEEL THE SAME WAY SOMETIMES...DON'T YOU FEEL LIKE ME? WE JUST HAVE THESE HABITS THAT WE'RE STUCK IN. AREN'T WE BRAINWASHED?"

He would then pause, and repeat what I said in the form of a question.

"Why are you stuck? Why are you brainwashed? Reflect on what you just said…who said you had to give up your choice. It seems to me that if you feel that strongly, you have a choice to walk away. Why not admit it and move on and find something else because obviously this is causing you pain. If I felt like you, I would just move on, maybe give it a rest 'cause it's agitating you…"

He followed with this great question.

"Do you want my blessing or permission to be angry?"

Yes! Both! I wanted him to tell me that my feelings were normal, permissible, that I was in the same boat with everyone else, and yes, that the whole Catholic thing was tedious. I could leave with no consequences. This religious checkmate or crossroad was a jumping off point to several memorable conversations that would last for several weeks. My fading commitment to religion was the opening salvo which gave both Bill and me an opportunity to talk about shared fears and values.

During one great conversation, I directly confessed to Bill about the seriousness of my unbelief. I asked him for direction.

"WHEN I'M IN CHURCH, I FEEL ANGRY, ANXIOUS," I TOLD HIM. "I FEEL ABOUT AS NONRELIGIOUS IN CHURCH AND AS REMOTE FROM GOD AS I CAN BE. WHAT THE HELL AM I DOING HERE? I'M JUST NOT CONNECTING TO THE CATHOLIC CHURCH THING ANYMORE. I FEEL NUMB; I DON'T CARE ABOUT IT. I'M NOT HAPPY TO ADMIT IT BUT CAN YOU UNDERSTAND THAT, OR TO PUT IT ANOTHER WAY, HAVE YOU HEARD THAT FROM A LOT OF PEOPLE?

"Some of it, of course. Maybe you're expecting too much from the Church—and from yourself," he counseled.

I ranted: "I EXPECT SOMETHING FROM THE CHURCH, BUT IT SEEMS LIKE I'M JUST PUTTING IN TIME. AND SO IS EVERYONE ELSE. IT'S LIKE THIS OBLIGATION THAT WAS BEAT INTO ME AND NOW IF I DON'T GO, I'VE GOT ALL THESE CONFLICTING FEELINGS. I GOT THE KIDS, GOT THE HOUSE, GOT THE PARISH. WHAT ELSE DO YOU DO?"

Sarcastically, in a humbling put down, he responded,

> *"I would think you're a little too old to be still wrestling with all of this. I would think you would have come to a conclusion one way or the other by now. If I was as turned off as you, maybe I'd try something else."*

Several times I had contemplated doing exactly that. I visited several other churches and even sat in a Quaker meeting. I concluded that I wasn't looking for another building or faith, but that I just didn't like my faith anymore. And I was convinced there wasn't any difference in any of the others. To me, they were all selling the same schtick.

> "I'M TELLING YOU," I RAISED MY VOICE, "IT'S LIKE THIS TORTURE THAT I CONTINUE TO PUT MYSELF THROUGH FOR A LOT OF REASONS AND YET I FEEL WORSE BY BREAKING AWAY FROM IT. IT'S CONFLICT INSIDE OF ME; I GOT THESE TWO VOICES FIGHTING. ONE SAYS, 'FORGET ABOUT IT, WASTE OF TIME,' THE OTHER SAYS, 'YOU BETTER BE CAREFUL; YOU'LL BE WORSE OFF WITHOUT IT.' IT'S AN INSURANCE POLICY IN A WAY. I GO ALONG BECAUSE I FEAR ANY ALTERNATIVES. DO I WANT TO DIE AND FIND OUT THEY WERE RIGHT AND I WAS WRONG?"

> *"That's normal,"* Bill assured me, *"and you are much too hard on yourself."*

> "BUT YOU DON'T HAVE THAT PROBLEM!" I SHOT BACK.

> *"How do you know?"*

> "SO YOU REALLY DO DOUBT AT NIGHT?"

> *"Yes, I wake up in the middle of the night and I have my worst doubts."*

> "SO WHY DO WE NEED THE CHURCH? EXCEPT OF COURSE, WHEN I'M SCARED, SICK, OR NEED TO BURY SOMEONE.

> *"It does help when people die to comfort folks,"* he argued. *"Where do you go when someone is sick or dying?"*

"Yeah, I get that. I said, "As soon as things are tough, I turn to God.""

"Okay so aside from the burial thing, why do we need big fancy churches and why are we supporting this big corporation if the only real benefit is a good place to bury people?

"All I can tell you is don't worry so much about the structure. You're focused only on the human part of it, which we can't change. It's probably always been that way. BUT, it's about community. It's about tradition. There's wisdom passed on to every generation. And wisdom is passed on through the life of the Church. I do believe that."

"Still," I insisted, "you're not answering why we just can't be nice to one another and forget this big fancy rich hotel you're living in that is paid for by a lot of collection plates."

Bill impatiently responded,

"You're too critical. That kind of thinking will just make you angrier. And I choose not to do that."

"Then answer me this—what difference does it make if I am a Catholic or not. What am I doing it for? Aren't I just going along because I'm weak and insecure and I need to because human existence is so damn frightening?"

"My faith helps me see things in a better light. It gives me hopeful eyes. And you're not seeing the hopeful aspect. I don't need all the answers."

I am a doubting Thomas. It's my middle name in fact. I need to put my hands in the wounds. But Bill pointed out that there was a lot I believed in that I didn't see.

"You can choose to believe or not to believe. You can choose to love, to hate, or, like me, I had to choose to live and not just live but to find new meaning in my life. And I choose to recognize God's presence in my life. It's my choice, but I also believe it's an innate part

of me. It's there all the time. I can choose to feel or look for God or not. I believe. That's it. I can't speak or answer anyone's unbelief. And though I've had my moments, I look for God everyday and I find him. I can't help an atheist. I've got nothing to say to convince anyone. It's in me."

That instinct made sense to me.

"SO ARE YOU SAYING THOSE DEEP, UNSPEAKABLE FEELINGS, LOVE, KIND-NESS, THOSE SORTS OF THINGS, ARE GOD?"

"Look at your best side. Isn't it the part of you that loves? Your best responses to life come out of love. And I believe that's God's tool for us. He gives us the resources, internally, to heal ourselves, and help others to heal. Remember my Don Burt image of broken pots. We're all in various states of brokenness and God gives us one an-other—and love—to help us mend the brokenness. I like that image. That's always worked for me."

"SO I SHOULD LOOK FOR GOD, AND GIVE GOD SOME CREDIT FOR THE GOOD STUFF?"

"Gratitude helps. The other view—anger, resentment, judgments—those feelings don't seem to get us anywhere. And what are your alternatives? Before you throw everything away that you were raised with, what are you going to replace it with? Science has suc-ceeded in pointing out a lot of fairy tales in religion. And religion is taking a back seat today, but we still search for truth. I'm just trying to understand. And I can't argue with a non-believer. I've got nothing to say that can disprove or prove anything. But no one has given me a suitable alternative. So I may doubt, I may still, at moments, un-believe, but by choosing God, I seem to be better. I'm better for myself and I'm better for others.

I conceded on the community part. That's one really sensible thing I picked up from the Augustinians. A community of believers.

"BUT EVEN THAT SOMETIMES GETS TIRING," I PROTESTED, "EVERYONE TALKS ABOUT COMMUNITY AD NAUSEM, BUT IT'S SO FRIGGIN' HARD TO IMPLEMENT."

"My Augustinian brothers, on a good day, help me to be more aware, in tune to one another. Joy, pain, we come together in both and it's better to celebrate together than to suffer alone. Imagine, my father dies, and no one calls, no one comes to his funeral. But I get comfort from my community."

Alright already. I get it. I should focus on God in my life, be more appreciative. He's there even if I don't choose to see Him. And a community of believers is better than a community of selfish cynics. So I left that day determined to live in a state of gratitude. Again, Bill's advice wasn't changing the course of human history. It wasn't the magic bullet or pill I wanted to swallow. But after an hour or so, between my venting and his easy listening, I felt better. But as I walked away I said to myself,

"Hey moron, why do you burden him with your nonsense? Stop whining at his door, wanting free, easy answers."

And that led to a simple gift he gave me:

"Live a life of gratitude."

Yes, a free, easy answer.

CHAPTER 7

THE NINTH LIFE

B ILL WAS LIKE A CAT WITH NINE LIVES. ALTHOUGH HE HAD BEEN CLOSE TO dying many, many times, he always seemed to find his way back. During his final year, however, he and I both sensed that things were different. He actually whispered to me one morning, "I don't think I'm beating it this time." With those words, he handed me the following poem:

"AT DEATH'S DOOR"
(January 2006)

At death's door, I stood one day
Just a visit, I did not stay
Crisis over, I gave a sigh
I think I was – afraid to die.

In a moment, life was altered
Glanced the future, almost faltered
I could not do the things I did
I think I was afraid to live.

Through these encounters, answers I sought
About life and death, I gave some thought
Faced the unknown, faith faded out
Fear stepped forward, so did my doubt.

Why did I doubt? Why did I fear?
Was I naïve? Or lacking in years?
Death's door again, question I ask
Would I be weak? As in the past?

Reflect I did, some thoughts anew
About my life, a broader view.
These thoughts hidden? Were they obscure?
An answered prayer and nothing more.

My life as is; is not my own
It belongs to Him, it's just a loan
Over the years, what did I learn?
Life is a gift, I did discern.

Another thing learned, I'm not alone
And some day now, He'll call me home
In life and death, His presence near
No room for doubt and less for fear.

And when He calls, with hope I pray
He's been with me along the way
Beyond death's door, with hope I pray
He's been with me along the way

Beyond death's door, for me He waits

With a smile and a long embrace.

I'm not afraid to admit that I fear death. I always have. It has always been an obsession for me. Surely, I know I'm just passing through, but that thought doesn't make me any less uncomfortable. As my favorite neurotic Woody Allen once said,

"I'm not afraid of death; I just don't want to be there when it happens."

Actually, as I've aged, I'm working on the acceptance part. I used to shake my head when I watched my mother read the newspaper death notices. Now, I do the same thing. It saddens me, though, to think that someday I'll have to leave my loved ones. And though I've been raised to believe that I'm going somewhere better, it offers me little comfort. Freud would have a field day with my unhealthy dose of fear, most likely asserting I had many unresolved childhood conflicts. I don't think I do. I just don't feel like leaving yet. And even worse, I fear a really, sudden stupid death. Random death makes me even crazier. The idea of being in the wrong place at the wrong time and being a victim of a senseless death, really keeps me up at nights. I've always been envious of people who don't appear worried about or fear dying. They seem, for whatever reason, to have their fear totally in check. In fact, some of my close friends who I've broached the subject with say they are resigned to the fact that we cannot do anything about dying, so why fear it?

When I discuss death openly with people, there are usually two clear camps. One group is emphatic that we're heading to dust, nothingness. That just flat out depresses me, pure and simple. Others have this rock solid faith that Jesus has gone ahead and is busy preparing a golden house for them. And the confidence with which they speak unnerves me.

Unfortunately, an explanation such as "He's up in heaven looking down on us," just doesn't comfort me. I have read everything I can get my hands on about death. I've searched all of the great philosophers, religious thinkers, and I keep coming up empty. I'm actually jealous of some people's unblinking self-assurance when it comes to death.

I like to talk about death, but it's not a subject you easily bring up. Even at funerals, it seems no one wants to talk about death. For that reason, whenever I can land any help with my own fear of dying, I jump at the opportunity. For as long as I remember, I'll listen to anyone's theory on how we got here and where we're going, and I take great comfort from anyone who speaks with authority on the subject.

Since I was morbidly obsessed with the subject, I began what were to be several long conversations with Bill about death in general terms and then about our own personal fears. It seemed to me that Bill, too, wanted to talk about death.

The very first time I explained to Bill about my fears, he told me that I wasn't really afraid of death; I was actually afraid of unprepared death.

"No," I insisted one day, "I'm afraid of all sorts of death, like when I see people dying those senseless deaths at the hands of terrorists or drunk drivers."

I asked Bill, as a priest first, how he handled the random deaths. If he had to preach at someone's funeral, perhaps a young child's, where did he find the strength, or more importantly, the words to comfort the victim's family? I confessed to Bill that this was one part of priesthood that I really respected. We may criticize, even dislike the clergy, but we do call on them during the really big event. Bill was very honest with me.

> *"I don't have any answers for you, so if you want to talk about something else, then you probably should," he instructed me.*

> "YOU DON'T WORRY ABOUT IT LIKE I DO, DO YOU?" I SHOT BACK.

> *"How do you know what I worry about?"*

> "IT DOESN'T SEEM LIKE IT," I SAID, "AT LEAST YOU WEAR A GOOD FACE."

> *"I have anxiety," he confessed. "Doctors have been on me to control my anxiety. Mostly, I have anxiety about breathing. Often I can't get my breath. Particularly in this last year, it's been very bad. I know I'm anxious when I don't get enough air. I'm not sure what I fear, but I'm fearful. I don't think I fear death. But you'll be happy to know that for years I feared death. I feared the separation from loved ones."*

Really? Bill worried? I was feeling better already. Another revelation that brought him down to my world! Wow, we were actually fearful of the very same thing. I admitted to Bill that I've been especially fearful since I've had children. I guess I'll be a bit more comfortable with my own death if I live to see them on their way. But I get very scared of thinking about my premature death and the effect it would have on my family.

"That's not crazy; that's normal," Bill said with labored breath.

"Maybe it is, but when I'm tossing and turning in the middle of the night, normal doesn't get me back to sleep."

"Me either. I hate the middle of the night. And if I wake up, forget it, I'm anxious."

"What do you think death will be like?" I continued.

Bill broke into a slight smile and explained his vision of death like he was just waiting for someone to ask.

"This isn't my idea so I won't take credit for it. Maybe it was my friend, Don Burt's idea. He has an image of a boat going over a waterfall. The waters are raging and the boat is dangerously almost capsizing in the turbulence. And then you fall, into a quiet, peaceful pool of water. I like that image."

I liked that image, too. Bill told me on several occasions that he would get very frightened when he had to be showered or bathed. Since he had no movement, he felt intensely the need to fight for breath when immersed in water. He told me that he often had the feeling that he was drowning and dreamt frequently that he was in situations where he was fighting to stay afloat. So we both reveled for a minute in the image of a calm, peaceful pool.

"What else helps you deal with death?" I continued.

"Again, I've taken some comfort from the words of Don. He also said, and I like this a lot, and this helps me too, that there are two things you can measure yourself with at the end of your life. How much you are loved and whether or not you are embraced by Christ in the end."

The first one I got. But what if Christ is just a fantasy? Just a nice fairy tale? What if there's nothing, nothingness. Don't all of us who bought into this religion thing get the royal shaft so to speak?"

"Sure," he said, "but I'll take my chances. I just don't like the alternative; I'd rather hope."

I agreed with him. When I look at all of the explanations that humans have come up with, the explanation that this life is all there is doesn't sit well with me. I want to believe that we are progressing to something greater. I like very much the concept of reincarnation where we continue to another plane of existence to work on the things we didn't do well in this life. But I didn't want to digress. Bill had the floor on death; I wanted to let him roll.

In a highly unusual moment, Bill took over the conversation completely. He wanted to keep talking about his own fear, so I sat back and enthusiastically listened.

"But anyway, at one time, I was afraid to live because of everything that happened, and getting through just one day was incredibly difficult. But back then I was also afraid to die. But I've had these encounters, lots and lots of time, being very close to dying. So it's giving me something to reflect on, these encounters with death or maybe God? And all the time, I faced each episode with doubt and fear, especially at 19 years old. At 19, I feared the unknown. And that stayed with me for a long, long time, that fear. It's still an unknown, but this last time I was almost out of here; I didn't have the same fear. Maybe because I'm getting older and the inevitable is upon me. Maybe I'm approaching death with cautious optimism. Life over the falls."

"Alright," I countered, "I get it, but let's go back to your other remark—what does it take to be embraced by Christ?"

I have a hard time with these kinds of expressions. I don't mean to be disrespectful, but I need this type of language clarified, specifically.

Bill answered,

> *"To me, it just means how well you stayed the course. The course being the calling to be the example Christ was. Once I went to a big meeting for the Order (a Chapter meeting). It lasted a few days and there were debates and discussions and philosophies and mission statements. After it was over, I'm riding my chair out of the room and someone asked me, 'What do you think we accomplished?'*

> *"My response has always been, and this is what I mean by the embracing part, that maybe it's not important that we accomplish anything; maybe it's only important that we tried. Tried to be faithful. Faithful to the calling of being a loving person in the example that Christ set forth. Faithful to family, friends, fellow human beings. And that's tough enough. I think we get all caught up with accomplishments and forget the simple things. Almost because the accomplishment part might be easier."*

Bill would always bring things back to the simplistic. Admittedly, he was not a theologian nor as he described himself, "a philosopher in any shape or form," but he always gave a concrete, common sense direction for people to follow. I asked him what he would say to a non-Christian or a non-believer?

> *"First of all, non-Christians or non believers don't seek my counsel, but I think I can stand on the principle that universally, be faithful to yourself. Whatever you deeply hold to be true, live it with conviction. Hopefully when we get down to it, we're all sitting in the same ballpark. Loving others. Being true to one another. That's a good human life lived."*

I referred back to his poem, once more asking, "In your position, is it harder to stay the course?"

> *"No. I'm still human, still have the same challenges as everyone else. Do I have self-doubt? Am I always certain? No. That goes with*

the unknown. I always ask God, and that's what my poem might be saying, to help me with my unbelief."

"AND WHAT DO YOU SAY TO AN ATHEIST?

"I've never given that any thought. I don't know if I can talk to a non-believer about faith or an afterlife. I only deal with what I believe. People have to come to their own conclusions based on their experiences. While we're on the subject of anxieties, let me give you another one of mine. I never anticipated this. I thought after 40 years in my condition, my next stop would have been the cemetery. Because they tell me I shouldn't have lived this long. I didn't think there was anymore God could ask me to let go. And today, I'm still battling things that are out of my control. God's still asking me to let go. I thought he threw everything at me that could be asked of a human to suffer. I really didn't think there was anything left and then He throws the kitchen sink at me. Sometimes people have said or asked in confession mainly, what was the thought provoking moment in my life. How did I cope with the disability and all the accompanying years of health problems? Bad news. I've got nothing profound. No light bulb went off with an answer. Just me sitting here all this time. What I tried to say in this poem is that as much as you think you can go through a crisis with your own self and your own abilities, that's not how it is. You can't. Some crises are just bigger than the individual. You need help. You know other people. And you lean on them. God never gives you a cross to crush you. I've heard that and I disagree. All crosses crush you. But what I've learned is that God sends you people to help you carry it."

Again, there was Bill's enduring theme, the juxtaposition of a crushing cross and angels coming to help lift your burdens. It was a line that Bill repeated often.

"Sometimes, people don't see the bleak side. They only see the bleak side when their life is not that bleak. They observe others, day in

and day out, and shake their heads, glad it's not them. I feel like shaking people sometimes. Wake up. Take notice. Extend a hand. Get out of yourself. Don't wait until a tragedy or a loss to take notice that your life is fleeting. Pay attention to God's presence in your life everyday and respond to others accordingly, with love. And sometimes, when life is kicking me in the teeth, all I can say to myself is tomorrow's a better day; today's a washout."

We had talked for well over an hour, and I could see Bill was very tired and that he politely was ending the conversation. He never liked as he said, "getting too heavy" but I was excited that we were talking about things deeper than the NBA. I asked him if I could come back and continue this death talk stuff and he nodded, "How about tomorrow?"

Leaving his room, I felt less fearful than when we first began the conversation. The next morning we picked up where we had left off.

"IF there is a special place with lots of provisional admission requirements, there's a good chance I won't get the acceptance letter and that just compounds my fears," I began.

Bill looked at me as if to say,

"I can't believe you're going to continue on this death stuff." He joked, "Why don't we just talk about the last movie you saw?"

"No, I like to talk about my fear and I love listening to how folks imagine death and an afterlife. It's one of those areas that if someone gives me a pleasant image, I'll walk around with it just for the comfort. Whenever I go to an art museum, I migrate to any painting depicting death or heaven or hell. Do you think I should be seeing someone professionally since I have this death fetish?"

"Absolutely!" he said, "I thought we covered it pretty well yesterday and you've got the poem, and I told you about my own fear so let's end with death is a part of life; there's nothing else left to say about it."

Bill was not in the mood to talk on the second day and he seemed impatient. I sensed that I should leave well enough alone. But all the talk of death from the day before raised a whole new set of questions for me. So I told Bill that I didn't have anything to talk about. I sat next to him and flipped on the television. We sat in silence watching CNN. I had learned that sometimes with Bill, I didn't have to talk. After years of trying to keep conversations going with senseless chatter, I was now able to sit and pass the time in silence. After several quiet minutes Bill spoke up.

"Are we going to work on the book?" he asked.

"I don't want to force a conversation if you're not feeling good."

"I'm okay," he said, "and it's funny, last night in the middle of the night, I laid awake thinking about our conversation yesterday."

"So did I! And guess what? I think you helped me with my death fear—so thanks."

I had wanted to continue the conversation from the day before. I had planned to ask Bill about the whole Catholic belief of the resurrection of the dead. The resurrection of Jesus and his believers is the central tenet of the religion, but honestly, I wanted his assessment of the concept.

"PERSONALLY, I LIKE THE NOTION OF ETERNAL HAPPINESS WITH GOD. I LIKE THE IDEA THAT I'LL RISE FROM THE DEAD," I STARTED. "BUT ETERNITY? FOREVER AND EVER? HEAVEN? HELL? RESURRECTION OF THE BODY? RESURRECTION OF THE SOUL? BIG THOUGHTS TO CONTEMPLATE! AT LEAST THEY ARE TO ME! PLEASE, YOUR TURN, COMMENT PLEASE," I PASSED OFF TO HIM.

"Look, I told you, I'm in the same boat. I guess I don't need the same assurances you do. And I don't think I can give you the answers that you want, and I suggest you go back and study, search to help you with your doubts. There is a point where you either believe or you don't. So I'm suggesting that you just focus on things that we do know," he replied. "Let's talk about something else."

Bill was having a lot of trouble breathing. I decided that it was selfish of me to continue to talk to someone in great discomfort, whose health was deteriorating rapidly. I was feeling a bit guilty for pressing him. Although he would have liked to continue with the conversation, he was kind enough to admit that he was feeling too weak. I could either sit with him while he slept or I could leave. Though I didn't want to admit to myself that Bill was dying, he seemed to be on a clear path to his end. I decided to just sit there while he slept. As I sat there I started to wonder whether or not this moment was by design. Was God allowing me to participate as a witness to the process of death in order for me to deal better with my own fear? Bill did teach me that I couldn't do anything about dying. but I could do a better job at living. As he dozed, I thought about the preciousness of time and made a commitment to myself not to waste the gifts given to me. I realized that my own healthy fear of death might be a good thing. Bill had taught me not to fear death itself but an unprepared death. Bill's message was to seize control over those things in life that enable you to look back with confidence, knowing that you worked to improve the world for others. It was one of the few moments in my life when I was at peace. He slept and I sat in a chair next to his bed contemplating a hope that one day, he and I would talk somewhere "over the falls" and joke about how my fears were childish and silly. Contemplating my death fear with Bill helped me to realize that it was not something to be ashamed of, but thinking and preparing for death was one of the most productive things I could do. For the first time in my life, I was able to compartmentalize this obsession and deal with it in a positive way.

Bill had accumulated nothing in his life as a priest. He had lived a life of poverty. Even the one physical possession he had, the use of his body, had been taken away from him. Bill taught me among many things, that despite my insecurity and fears, attachment to life's possessions was unhealthy and would only leave me more fearful. His faith was the tool that enabled him to deal with his realistic assessment of his own life. Bill left life with the essence he cultivated throughout his entire existence on earth. Patience and love for others, compassion for those who suffer, were his motivations for continuing his life when most of us would have despaired. I didn't bring up death again but several days later on Ash Wednesday, Bill brought closure to our earlier conversation.

> "This is an important day in the Church and one that always made sense to me," he said. "This should be a big day for you," he quipped out of the side of his mouth. "It's a good reminder that we're on a journey, and we begin the journey with nothing and leave with nothing but our soul. So cultivate the good things about yourself and take them with you as you continue your journey."

CHAPTER 8

LOOKING BACK

A WEEK OR SO AFTER OUR RECENT CONVERSATION ABOUT DEATH, I RETURNED to Bill's room assuming we had exhausted all possible topics for his book. I was also worried that these interviews were becoming too demanding on him physically. Looking at him propped up in bed, however, with some decent color returned to his face, I hoped he was starting to feel like his old self again. But he wasn't. I didn't want to admit it, but he was in his final stages of life. His body was experiencing a systematic breakdown. Next to Bill's bed was a machine that chirped and beeped, keeping count of all of his vital signs, and Bill was acutely aware of all of them.

The amount of oxygen being carried in his blood was low and he now wore a cumbersome oxygen mask all the time. If I asked him a question that he wanted to answer, however, he would ask me to lift the mask so I could hear his answer. His voice had grown faint, and on this particular morning he greeted me by remarking,

"This doesn't look good, does it?"

After years and years in a wheelchair, lasting well beyond all the doctors' predictions, Bill's body was giving out. The years of stress had taken their toll, and a blinking machine's bleak statistics now drove home the reality of his approaching death.

"All that talk of death and dying jinxed me," he jokingly quipped, knowing how quickly I could feel guilt. "Did I give you what you wanted?"

Amazingly he was still interested in the book idea and actually seemed to be fishing for a compliment.

"It was great talking about death," I said sarcastically, "I was joyfully depressed for the past week."

Although straining at the effort, he smilingly replied,

"I want to make sure I give you some good stuff."

I suddenly realized that Bill had finally fully embraced my original motive, which was to capture a piece of him for posterity. Though each moment for him had become a struggle, he seemed like he wanted to pursue conversation like never before. Fearing I would add more strain to the situation, I tried not to impose any more questions on him. In fact, by this time, I wasn't concerned about conducting another interview or finishing the book for that matter. Actually, for one rare moment, it was I who sat in silence. Very unusual. Sitting there, the thought hit me that I was sharing in his death. I was hopeful that he still had some time, but my gut told me the end was approaching quickly. I was sad. Watching someone breathe on a machine, breath to breath, moment to moment, made me focus on the enormity of the moment. Watching Bill struggle for a breath made me wonder what he himself was thinking.

Bill sensed my pensiveness and pointed to me to remove his mask. He assured me he could talk for several minutes without it.

"What, no questions today?"

Nope, I had nothing to say. I couldn't muster up the courage to say what I was thinking, namely,

"Bill, you're dying, and guess what? I'm going to miss you."

These feelings surprised me. In this very strange way, we had grown close. And here we were, neither one of us with the capacity to acknowledge or express any intimate feelings. But I was feeling sad and truthfully, I was amazed at how sad I felt. This wasn't my best friend, but as I sat there I contemplated the long relationship we had shared.

Suddenly, I just blurted out, "Hey, how about looking back?"

"What?" he asked.

"Look back. Over your life. Do you have any regrets?"

"You want to talk about regret?"

"Not really. I just said that to fill up the space. But I was just wondering, if you <u>were</u> looking over your past, is there anything you'd do differently?" I asked. "I guess I want to know if you feel like you missed out on something."

> *"Don't you think everyone has regrets?" he asked me. "But it's like all fears—they're not based on anything that makes sense. You can't go back and change anything, right?"*

Ironically, I told him I spent hours obsessing about missed opportunities, times I should have zigged instead of zagged. And after fifty, my obsessions were getting worse.

> *"I meditate a lot," he responded, "and I try not to dwell on mistakes and I try to focus on the positives. I make myself think good thoughts if I can. If you want to talk about death, I think meditating about it is good. Do you ever think that because you think about it a lot that maybe you're more aware and appreciative of the time you have?"*

❧

Bill was right. I had become increasingly aware and at least partially appreciative that I was now on the back nine of my own life. Life slowly and quickly crept up on me now. For years every moment of my waking hours was taken up with some activity involved in raising a family and working. I rarely had the time to give my own mortality much more than a cursory thought. I was so preoccupied with my own trivial pursuits that I pushed my own ending out of mind. Being a spectator to Bill's dying made my own more palpable.

Bill must have sensed that I needed a lesson that day since he whispered, "Appreciate those around you. Appreciate today."

Again, that always bothered me. How do I do this? I've got responsibilities, kids, bills, demands on me. I don't have time to appreciate. I half jokingly responded, "That's easy for you to say; you're not me."

He reiterated, "Dwell on appreciation—you have to. You have to make time to appreciate."

Bill's instruction reminded me how I once asked Father Shawn Tracy, a fellow Augustinian of Bill's, why he always seems in a good mood. He is always a happy kind of guy. And he told me that he's always happy because he knows he will die. Bill was quietly, almost silently teaching me the importance of preparing for my own death. Not in a morbid way but by living a life of gratitude.

"Here's a practical thing I do every time I wake up and can't get back to sleep," he explained. "I start with the earliest pleasant memory of the first person I can think of. I can usually conjure up something from about year three of my life. And then I imagine one good thing that happened to me each year. I think about each year in school and so on. Soon I'm smiling and then quickly I'm back to sleep and feeling relaxed, happy."

I liked that meditation idea and since that time I've incorporated it into my ritual and I credit Bill with getting me back to sleep many evenings since.

"I'm leaving, you're leaving, simple as that. The body is staying and we are going," he said. "So don't look back, look forward."

"ME? GOING FORWARD. LIKE MY ESSENCE?"

"Your soul. It's going."

"LIKE WHAT? LIKE I'M JUST TAKING MY ACCUMULATED SELF WITH ME?"

"That's the faith part. And you're leaving behind something of yourself to all who knew you. And I always have told people that if you live with patience and love, you'll be happy here and that's what you'll take. If you live a good life, and you believe that, you can

move on without fear. Don't waste a lot of energy looking back with regret. If you must look back, remember all the pleasant times."

That helped! In a very brief moment of calm, Bill softly spoke a great lesson. Fight anxiety with gratitude. Consciously take time out of the day to say thank you.

"Why torment yourself over the failures; focus on the good you did," he continued. "There's probably more of that than you give yourself credit for and it's okay to pat yourself on the back once in awhile."

I cultivated for years the habit of self criticism. Judging myself. Looking back with regret. Wishing I had made different choices in my life and in my career. Microscopically, I zoom in on all of my faults. Did I get on the wrong boat? Maybe too much conformity? Afraid to take chances? Always, playing life safe? And dwell and dwell on my mistakes. Especially in terms of the people I've hurt. I'm very conscious of those situations with others in which I have failed or the million times I proclaimed harsh judgments against my enemies. The silver lining of this conversation was the surprise that Bill admitted to doing much the same thing.

"Believe it or not, I sometimes do the same thing but maybe not to the extent you do," he teased.

"I guess lots of people would want to know if I wish I could have gone back and lived my life with movement, without the accident," he said. "But really, the thing I regret is the people I've hurt."

"YOU'VE HURT PEOPLE? I CAN'T IMAGINE WHO."

"Sure, I know I have, and if I could go back I'd try and undo that."

"THAT MAKES ME FEEL BETTER. I DIDN'T THINK YOU HAD ANY SKELETONS IN YOUR CLOSET EXCEPT ALL THE TIMES YOU GAVE ME SHIT."

"Oh yeah, I've got some. Once I heard an interview. It was an athlete, retired with bad knees and ankles. He could hardly climb the stairs. He was asked the same question that you asked, 'Any regrets?' He said, 'If I had one wish and could go back in time, I'd

say I'm sorry to someone I hurt.' *I'd do the same.*"

"WELL THAT'S AMAZING. SO EVEN YOU HAVE FLAWS?"

"Of course."

"GIVE ME ONE!"

"People have told me that I'm not good at taking compliments."

"THAT'S A FLAW?"

"Looking back on my life, I've received lots of awards. Awards make me uncomfortable. They give me an award because I've been paralyzed? Makes me uncomfortable. And maybe I should have been more enthusiastic in my accepting that type of thing."

"MAYBE," I COVERED. "YOU PLAYED A BAD HAND SO WELL AND THAT MAKES PEOPLE TAKE NOTICE."

"Maybe. And I don't speak up. That's something else I don't do well. I assume others know more than me."

"BUT YOU KNOW A HELLUVA LOT."

"I know I'm patient; that's a strength of mine."

"IS THAT YOUR BIGGEST STRENGTH?"

"Now that you're forcing me to look back, it wasn't always. I've had to learn to be patient."

That's the one thing I had observed over all the time I had known him. The patience. The endless waiting. Waiting for this one or that one to come in and do this or that. And if people didn't show up to help him, he waited some more. Waiting to get dressed, waiting to get fed, waiting for someone to open a door. Patience the size of Mount Everest. Suddenly, I wasn't sad. I was sitting next to him looking back on his life with admiration and feeling joy that I knew him. I dwelled on the thousands of times I witnessed him, just patiently waiting. For days. Laying still, just waiting.

"You're Superman," I said. "I'm going to force you to take a compliment from me. You got superhuman strength and being around you makes me better," I followed.

He smiled an ever so slight self satisfactory smile. He seemed genuinely grateful that I had noticed. It was a proud accomplishment.

After a moment or so I asked, what's the one thing, the thing in your mind that stands out, the thing you want to be remembered for?

"You tend to give me too much credit," he said. "All my guidance, I got from others. There has always been some key person I can go to and rely on. Just because I'm in a wheelchair doesn't mean I got the answers. I'll have to think about that for a bit. But I will tell you when I think of it. When I was in the seminary in Staten Island, it was a nuthouse. A full five years where at that time, people were coming and going. You're studying Greek wondering what you're doing and people up and leave. You need others to clarify things for you sometimes; you can't find answers by yourself. No man's an island? That's probably it. My life is proof that no man is an island. Is that something I'll be remembered for?"

"YOU CAN COME UP WITH SOMETHING BETTER THAN THAT!" I BEGGED.

"I appreciate your compliment that I played a bad hand well. But everyone gets a bad hand at some point. I guess I want to be remembered as a person who was true to what he believed in. A person who could be counted on to find the good in others even when sometimes he struggled with that. Like I said earlier, you are your essence and to discover that and to appreciate your own uniqueness is a great purpose. Fear, insecurity, unrealistic expectations of life and others? My injury made me deal with me and me alone. I couldn't be all the other things that people struggle with. I couldn't worry or compete to be rich or accomplished. My struggle has always been to be more genuine, more real, more myself. Is this helping?"

Yes, it was helping. All of my visits were helping. Learning from Bill that

I should trust my instincts. Believe in the deeper things in life. Role play less; be true to my beliefs. The past year had been a slow process of peeling off layers one after another. Mutually helping one another to forgive ourselves for our faults and be thankful for our gifts. Bill helped me greatly accept the movements of life's pendulum. He taught me the pragmatism that the bad, no matter how bad, can be negotiated, and daylight follows even the darkest nights.

On this day, I had taxed Bill more than I planned. I apologized for overstaying and having him talk more than he was supposed to.

"That's alright," he said. "I enjoy these talks."

"I'm glad. Me too."

I got up to leave and I reached out my hand to shake his.

"You know," he said.

"What?"

"You know what your gift is, Steve?"

"My gift?"

"Your gift is your ability to disarm people."

"That doesn't sound good."

"It's good. You disarmed me. And not many people can do that."

I wasn't entirely sure that was a compliment. For a moment I felt that maybe he meant that I probed too deep or was insensitive keeping boundaries. So I asked.

"Is that a real, certifiable compliment? Like something I can always remember that you like about me?"

"Yeah, it's a good thing. You should do more with that gift."

I chuckled and said, "Thanks" and left the room. It was a very good day.

CHAPTER 9

THE SAINT THING

URING HIS LIFETIME, BILL DEVELOPED A LOCAL SAINTLY REPUTATION. AS A result, when I first conceived the idea of writing a book with Bill, I thought, "Wow! What a great idea! A paralyzed priest, brimming with experiences! I'll just let him talk, and a plethora of inspirational ideas will just pour out! Alongside *Tuesdays with Morrie* on countless bookshelves, readers would be able to find the newest bestseller, *Mondays and Wednesdays with Father Bill!* As I confessed earlier, I had visions of being the first kid on the block to preserve a piece of a modern day saint. But as luck would have it, I hadn't counted on interviewing a reluctant wet blanket who would prove these initial assumptions completely wrong.

Good effort, misguided aim.

That's why I still look back in amazement on the last year of Bill's life. We traveled so very far together in a rather short time, and during that time, I reached one very large conclusion—my image of sainthood was just plain ass backwards.

First, let me explain that growing up Catholic, saints played a big role in my formative years. From my very first days of Catholic school, saints were embossed onto my brain. Each Friday afternoon in school, usually right after lunch, the nuns would read us a story from the *Lives of the Saints*. Usually the stories were about heroic figures. Saints were those men and women of Church history who had battled paganism and faced martyrdom for their love of Christ. The message was clear. These folks were not like you and I. They were larger than life itself. They had a divine something flowing in their veins that enabled them to go beyond ordinary human response. My own religious imagination was filled with these entertaining and enticing stories of ancient men staring down lions or being burned at the stake. My own "patron saint," Stephen, was stoned to death for having the unfortunate name of "Christian" on his résumé. I strongly doubted that I could follow that act.

Saints in Catholicism are a big deal! And becoming a saint is no ordinary matter. It's a fairly involved and costly process that follows very rigid guidelines. And the last time I checked, there needs to be a few documented miracles attributed to the candidate for sainthood during the canonization process (although the Pope can waive this requirement for a super special case).

When I first met Bill, I had been conditioned by so many people to believe he belonged in this extraordinary category. According to the devout people closest to Bill, he epitomized a life of exceptional holiness. Unfortunately, for many years I didn't feel this same "saint vibe." Extraordinary? Absolutely. No one could deny that Bill was remarkable. But a saint in the mold of my Friday afternoon *Lives of the Saints* stories? No way!

At the risk of sounding like a simpleton or a bit dense, for a long, long time (before our interviews began), I was actually disappointed with the saint comparison. Maybe it was because I was comparing Bill to the classic saint mold in my head. I jokingly asked one day,

"Do you have any miracles that you know of that you're keeping from me? Don't you think they would really help sales of your book?" Deep in the recesses of my subconscious, I harbored illusions of sitting with the Pope and handing him a copy of Bill's book. "Here, Holy Father, it was all my idea!" I was already anticipating my finder's fee from Rome for discovery and documentation of a real day modern saint!!

Bill laughed, but he didn't entirely discount my question.

"Maybe." he chuckled, "We don't know always know these things, do we? Maybe someday."

"Do you see yourself as a saint?" I then asked him, point blank.

"We're all called to be saints," he responded quietly. "I don't think God wants us to go around feeling great about ourselves just because we lead a good life. That's what His plan is for everyone. But living a life committed to Christ? I hope I've been true to that.

"People say now—and you know they'll say later—that you're a saint. There will be people who will make you one officially."

"Well you and I know that I'm just like everyone else."

"You're not! No way. You're definitely not like everyone else."

"If you say so."

"Truthfully, you've got something that I've never seen."

It was a good topic. Sainthood. Even though Bill would deflect any sort of compliment, I wanted him to know that at least in everyone else's eyes, his suffering would always be remembered and honored. I also felt like telling him that he took way too long to let me see it, but by then I realized that I was the guilty one for not accepting what I saw in him.

"You should be a saint, and if I get a vote, you're in," I insisted. "It's an incredible life you've lived. And now that you've convinced me, and I'm a tough guy to convince, then I'm telling everyone."

He shook his head and wryly replied, "I won't be here, but maybe you can throw a party."

Late in 2006, my regular visits with Bill had now become a waiting game. It was clear that his time was dwindling down quickly. His energy level was so low that I couldn't continue to bother him; he tired after just a few words. His failing health had me beginning to let go of the book idea. It was fun while it lasted but like so many ideas, it got postponed by reality. Execution is the death of so many creative impulses and circumstances seemed to be conspiring to kill this one too. I even tried to talk myself out of the idea completely.

"Too little, too late!" I said disappointedly aloud to myself as I walked back to my office. "We're just not going to get it done."

Later, in a melancholy, I consoled myself that I wasn't meant to be a biographer in the first place. And now at least, I wouldn't have to worry about getting Bill "right" or face that feared critic admonishing me,

"You didn't really know him like I did."

Bill had now become so weak that he could hardly speak. The tone of my visits changed. Once he may have politely tolerated my intrusions, but he now seemed to genuinely want me to visit. Ironically, though, there was almost no conversation except for a polite greeting. Normally, I'm very uncomfortable in the presence of someone's suffering. When I feel helpless, I want to fix a situation and if I can't, I quickly exit. It is a bad characteristic of mine. But I didn't feel this way now. I couldn't do anything to help him and yet it seemed like visiting—just sitting still— was action enough. Even my habit of incessant filling of the silences stopped. I was always very sociable and light hearted when times were good, but I normally hid from awkward situations of another's discomfort. But here, it seemed I was finally learning that the most important gift I could offer Bill was just some moments. Time was the gift I could give. I had often heard the phrase "to be present to another" but I never contemplated exactly what that meant. Probably because I didn't have the patience to do it. But here, both of us were content just to sit in silence, and "be present in the moment with one another." And, of course, a television in the room helped fill up the other moments. Now all my visits included watching the news or the movie channel. How we both loved watching those classic films!!

For the next several weeks, we sat in silence, watching favorites like "North by Northwest" or "Rear Window." We both loved Alfred

Hitchcock. After about two hours, Bill would quietly nod off, and I'd make my exit. Sadness overcame me. I would soon be losing a friend. A close friend I never knew I had. He was about to die.

After several such visits, though, Bill wasn't entirely comfortable with my new found quiet demeanor. One day he seemed to recapture a fraction of his old energy and suggested under labored breath that I could write some questions if I wanted and he would try to answer them when I wasn't around. He could tell from my half-hearted "maybe" that I had lost some of my fervor and who knows, he may have been trying to give me a necessary jump start. It must have been instinctual on his part, or at least a mechanism to get me talking when he asked, "What did you get out of all of this, Steve?"

"Out of what?"

"All the talking."

I laughed and said, "You'll have to hang around long enough to see." And then, as my last official question to him, I turned Bill's query back around on him.

"What did you get out of all of this, Bill?"

In a soft voice that I had to move closer to hear he said, "You made me reflect and answer a lot of things I probably just would have left alone."

"Is that a good thing or a bad one?"

"It was good. I didn't think so at the beginning, but I'm kind of used to it by now.

"Did I convince you that you're a saint?"

"No."

"I disagree. Bill, you are a saint. And I will tell you exactly what I got out of this—at least I've learned what it means to be a saint and you showed me."

Bill's mouth broke into a slight smirk and I sensed that my compliment meant a great deal to him. His life was one of true heroic saintliness. Braver than sitting in a den of lions. Not in the sense of the larger than life heroic deeds that were read to me in elementary school but in the way he managed his suffering. Bill surrendered to the will of God. Though I personally argued with him many times that he was a victim of very bad luck, Bill believed deep down that there was a reason for everything, and his job didn't necessarily include finding out that reason. He simply believed. His conviction was to follow the example of Christ, living a life of simple holiness. No matter what life threw at him, and everyday it threw something, he trudged through with great humility and patience.

Since Bill's death, I've told many people that Bill gave me the chance to see God. He didn't magically wipe out all my doubts; I still have many. But he lived in a place of gentle peace and tried every day to bring that peace to others. No, he wasn't perfect, but as I got to know him, the way he lived was pretty darn close. As I mentioned, I got a sense of what the apostles must have felt when they first met Jesus. This was not your ordinary man on the street. He was touched by God. Sainthood, holiness? Yep. The kind that makes you drop everything and follow someone? Yep. It just took me a lot of years to develop my vision.

CHAPTER 10

SOME GOOD BILL TALKING

THIS BOOK TRULY WAS A LABOR OF LOVE. OFTEN, WHILE TYPING BILL'S WORDS into my computer, I could almost hear his voice instructing, counseling, joking, or offering me encouragement. I tried to capture major themes of what Bill and I discussed while we planned for his book—the one that that did NOT get written.

I spent a great deal of time recording interviews with Bill, resulting in reams of transcripts. Some were filled with golden gems of wisdom; others were total snoozers. My editor, however, advised against publishing them word-for-word. I quite agree. To do so would be way too boring for the general reader.

Since my effort here, however, is a tribute to a remarkable man I thought it would be appropriate to allow Bill the last word from these interviews. And so, I have included some of Bill's quotes, verbatim, that capture his spirit, his spirituality, and some very random views about life in general.

HUMILITY

Bill and I often talked about the virtuous life and what it took to live a good life. On the top of Bill's list was humility.

> *"I always liked Augustine's take on the subject, namely, the way to God is first through humility, and then the second way is through humility and then the third way is through humility. It's an important virtue and one that we should really pay attention to…I don't think of humility as beating yourself up, but*

more that, I should try to face the truth about myself. I'm just average, maybe a little below. But our humble self is our better self, I think. Our proud, boastful self makes us a little danger-ous. That's what I get from Jesus. That's the ultimate humility. He hung out with sinners. He was no better than them.

"*I think we tend to get caught up in our own self-importance. I think that's a mistake. It very important for us to know that we're just passing through and that we're not steering the ship. God is. Humility is a good habit to cultivate. My good friend and mentor Don Burt preached one time that as human beings we're cracked, damaged. Augustine talks about life being fragile as glass. Humility helps to smooth out the cracks. It doesn't come natural, not even for me. I can be proud, stubborn. Again, to me humility fights ego and that can keep us from falling in love with power and control because, and I'm a great example, we're not in control. Jesus said 'The meek will inherit the earth.' That's practical advice. If you realize that you're no better than any other human, you treat everyone with value. That makes the quality of your life better. And too, not getting caught up in your own self-centered world makes you a nicer person to be around. And I speak from a position where I've been held captive for hours by self-centered people and believe me, it's trying.*"

POLITICIANS

One day I was in a particularly political mood. I was listening to some bad news one particular morning and asked Bill to sum up his political outlook and persuasion.

"*I'm not a conservative, not a liberal. I just sort of fend off be-cause I really don't know much of what we should do anyway. When I listen to the news, investigations of senators and repre-sentatives taking bribes, worse on lower levels probably, I won-der how many years that took to unfold. I'm not cynical. I just encourage people to become honest in their dealings and we'll become better. Politicians, it seems to me, are the quickest people to forget where they came from or who made it possible for them to be in office. I think it's very difficult to run a country, but today we're hearing a lot more bickering between parties than I think I've ever heard. The system, democracy, demands compromise and from what I'm watching there doesn't seem to be much. Maybe because it doesn't sell. Our politics are contentious 'cause it makes good television and politicians are now playing more to the cameras than to the people."*

≈

CHURCH AND STATE

On this topic, Bill was resolute!

"I really think, we've gone too far from mentioning God, or being a God-based, religious society. Correct me, if I'm wrong, but the original intent (of our forefathers) was that the state shouldn't impose a state religion on anyone. I think today we're mixing things up and interpreting that you just can't mention God anywhere in the political scene without a consequence. I'm not advocating pushing it down anyone's throat but the notion of a higher power in practice keeps us within some boundaries with one another. I think we've lost a great deal just in the way we treat each other. Worshipping the state leads us down a dangerous road, especially in a capitalist society. Again, I'm no expert but I've don't think we're as nice as we used to be. And as a society we're obsessed with consuming and getting ahead and we're not concerned enough, in my opinion, for those in our society who are not as fortunate. That's why the Church is important. Our institutions, though imperfect, play a role in keeping our consciousness raised. Keeping us focused on justice."

❧

SOCIAL JUSTICE

Bill taught a course in social justice so I thought he might offer some valuable insight on the subject.

> *"I only teach the course, I'm not an expert. What do they say—*
> *'an expert is only two pages ahead of everyone else.' I think*
> *many people I've witnessed think social justice is something*
> *extra that they can do in their spare time. In reality, justice is*
> *the minimum amount of love you owe to another person. The*
> *crisis is that people think, 'If I have the time, I'll donate,' but it*
> *should be more basic than that. Race, class? How to treat every-*
> *one as equals? Difficult. Bush declared a war on terrorism. In*
> *my life, I've seen a war on literacy, poverty, drugs, and guess*
> *what, we haven't won one war yet. We didn't win any of the*
> *above. We don't get it. The rich really do get richer when they*
> *already have too much. When they are totally indulged, maybe*
> *they'll give back. At the very least, we should believe that every*
> *citizen is entitled to literacy and health. I think this is where the*
> *Church needs to focus its efforts. We need to convince Catholics*
> *or educate them that Christ calls us to a life of activism. When*
> *we see wrong we work to right it not just showing up for*
> *Church and think everything is wonderful."*

❧

THE AMERICANS WITH DISABILITIES ACT
(AND THE RIGHTS OF THE DISABLED)

Many, many times over the course of my years with Bill, we talked about his awareness that developed as an adult with a disability. I often bugged him that he should be in the forefront of the disability movement because of his very visible public position, but he preferred people discover equality on their own without him hemming and hawing at them.

"People are just unaware of the disabled person's needs. You get the people who talk loudly at you? They're just unaware, lack experience. It frustrates others around me, but not me. The only time I was frustrated was this one time I went to a golf club for a reception. We called ahead and they said that they had a ramp. The ramp was on the normal stairway and let's just say it took 4 people to get me up this steep ramp.

"I confronted the manager that the club was not in compliance. A friend, who was a member of the club, was with me. The member said to me later, 'Frankly Bill, to tell you the truth, they don't want you here.' That was an eye opening experience. Ironically since then, they installed an elevator. But 'they don't want your kind,' is still very real.

"Over my life time have things gotten better? There's more awareness. More exposure. Thirty years ago, I was on the boardwalk. Maybe I'd see one other person in a wheelchair. Today, on a given day, I'll see 30. You want to ask a disabled person about quality of life? Measure their attendance at a facility or event. That will tell you if the facility or institution is up to speed. Personally, I haven't felt real injustice. Movie theaters have asked me to get out of my chair and out of an aisle. People see the disability first. Adults see disability, get uncomfortable. Children don't. On the boardwalk when I see kids, I smile; Kids will wave; mom and dad say, 'Don't disturb him.' Disabled people need opportunity, not pity. But that requires a commitment. Money. And then that's where the problem begins. But attitude and acceptance don't cost anything."

～

CHRISTIAN FAITH

As I've repeated many times to this point, we had an ongoing debate between my doubts and his faith. But here he simplifies and summarizes.

"I was taught to make a distinction between faith and formula. Let's go back to what we talked about before. The crux of my own faith is that there is a God. It's my gut instinct. I feel it. Not way out there. But a personal thing. And I believe, He steps into our history as the person of Jesus. That's what I was taught and that's what I believe.

"The bottom line is that I'm not speaking to a God way out there, but I can speak to one right next to me. Saying that, I never bought into the idea that there is no salvation outside the Church or outside of Christianity. Things have to be constantly reinterpreted for a new age. Take women priests. It's a closed subject, right? Not good theology. It's the same as slavery. Barring women does not hold up. There is no theological basis for it. As long as there is a theological reason, then I can support it. But where in scripture does it forbid it? And tradition is part of revelation. It is a source for us, a place we look for God.

"I'm not a theologian. Just a simple believer. Or I mean, I'm simply trying to be a believer. I always like to say or think that the reasons for us coming together is to be of one heart and mind (Augustine). It's just a goal. Over the years, I've had the opportunity to look at many others and their faith or lack of it. Let's just say we're on different paths. And that's okay with me."

HELL

QUESTION: BILL, AM I GOING TO HELL AND IS IT HOT THERE?

"I think God understands the trials and the effort to believe. Get another concept. Don't kill yourself trying to make perfect sense of all of it. Look at the world as a beautiful place. Look at the good, try and live and appreciate the goodness. That's where the hope comes in. Someday maybe we'll understand the purpose, but we can't comprehend it. It's a mystery but we're all

connected in the mystery. I don't believe God condemns us. God does not condemn us to anywhere. He gives us what we want. I always felt that we can choose God or choose ourselves. God lets us do either; this is free will. If we decide on ourselves and what we want, then God lets us. If we choose Him, then I think He comes into our lives. Eternity with Him comes from consistently choosing Him. And I think hell is eternity with ourselves.

"There's no absolute proof but like St. Paul said, 'Faith is believing in the evidence of things not seen.' Or something close to that. I feel something deeply. It's part of me. I didn't ask to feel it. It's just there. Someday I'll have an answer, I hope. But in the meantime, living scared for hell makes no sense. Don't live for a reward anyway. Live a good life because it makes you happy here on earth. That's its own reward."

RANDOM GUT STUFF

"I've always (as a young person) been in never-never land. Not thinking, not reflecting. After my accident, those months of being in bed, I saw the value of being alone (I had no choice, but a value nonetheless). I've had lots of time to reflect on what was important. You go through your teenage years; you push people out who infringe on your time and space. After I got hurt these same people were there to help me, especially my family. So be careful who you push out. All these people came and encouraged me not to give up. I get tired, want to give up.

"Getting off the ventilator is work. Each breath is conscious; it's not second nature. And sometimes it's really tough to keep at it. You want to just give up and say, 'Ok God, just take me. I'm off the vent for about an hour.' I try to keep my mind on other things other than the clock. Last time I was in the hospital, I was in and out of it. I would say, 'It's okay to leave me out of it.' Vent went off, I blacked out; people revived me. I said it was better to

let me go. Don't bother. But I'm glad I got to see another day. I try to reflect on different times, different friends, memories, good memories. A form of meditation. People come in, takes my mind off the time. But weird, I still enjoy the private quiet time. People ask, 'Are you getting cabin fever?' My whole life has been training for cabin fever. When I was young, in school, and we'd have a snow day. Even in the seminary during a snow day, people were like caged animals. I always was okay at those times. I always thought that in later years, the most time you'll spend is with yourself. So it's a huge advantage to get to know yourself. I thought in those early years, I didn't mind being by myself and now I find that I'm all the time by myself. I don't mind the self reflections; I don't scare of myself 'cause I'm still getting to know myself. I'm still saying stupid things. Just when you start to believe what people are saying about you, like that I'm a man of patience, I find out that I'm not patient at all. I want to quit; I say to myself, 'You're supposed to be a man of courage, where is it?' Or I still find myself being selfish, asking, what's in it for me? Nurses, they're qualified, but I don't like how they handle me. I actually yell. Like really yell. Hurt their feelings. So I deal with that and the truth of myself just like anyone else.

"And there are moments I'm not willing to fight the battle. I was in a mall with John Ryan. I almost got hit by a car. John Ryan screams to the driver, 'Everyone's in a f—-ing hurry.' I get to my van and two girls drive into a handicap spot. John corrects them and I let it go. One girl says, 'I've got a limp' and fakes a limp. He sends her a ticket in the mail. I say a prayer for her. I tend to let things go and maybe keep the anger in. Take it out on someone later when it's easier. My line in the sand is when I tell someone over and over the same thing and they don't do it. I raise my voice. On another note, being an Augustinian has helped. Other people in my spot don't have what I have had. When I first came in the seminary, I sensed bitterness; people

were angry because they didn't get certain positions or jobs or recognition. I always said, 'Whatever happens, I won't be bitter or resentful.' After the accident I was.

"When I first entered into this life I was given gifts and I wanted to use them. Those gifts were taken away. But God doesn't take away; He keeps giving. The gifts I lost, He said to me, 'You don't need those gifts for this journey; you'll need these instead.' And then He sent me the gifts I needed to do this journey. So what I'm saying is the cross is a gift or a loss. You have the power to decide."

~

VOCATION

"I can only speak about my experience. I've always observed in the priesthood the tension between the pastoral and the powerful. It's a real problem in the Church. It's always irritated me when my brothers used more power than pastoral in their approach to problem solving. And it's really critical that as ministers we approach the people we serve as pastoral ministers. Throughout my life, many times decisions were approached like a sledgehammer. I'd say to people, 'Let's do it this way', in a pastoral sense. But because people have position or perceive they are important and in charge, they can slam the door. Makes the problem go away in the short run. But it also makes people fall into habits of going along. You don't really build anything. You just exert your will in the short term. I always found if you can take everyone's point of view into consideration and do your best to build consensus, you've got a better chance at building compromise. Which ultimately, that's how things move forward. A lot is related to our own egos.

"Most of the people I'm preaching to don't have a power position.

The power people rarely hear what they need to hear. The problem with power is the people want it, get it, and don't want to give it up. But in the end, we know, it does us no good. In the end, we have to let go. We die. So power over others is just an illusion. Personally, I'm afraid of power. I could have been that way. Maybe if I didn't have my accident, I could have gone for power. My physical power was taken away."

∾

PENANCE

On one particular day, I was very critical of the idea of confession. I was forced for years to attend and I always resented it. Bill had a tonic for that too.

"I think Jesus is like a signpost or a benchmark. Call it what you want but a yardstick to measure ourselves. He presented us with an authentic model for being human. We always fall short but I believe this is the way to God—by following Jesus' example. I can't help you with your trouble with the sacrament. I can only speak about forgiveness. I have found out in my life that I always thought that God forgave me. But I've learned the toughest person to forgive is yourself. I have a hard time forgiving myself, letting go of my imperfection. Penance sometimes can help with that. Maybe it's just a really effective psychological device. Don't think about it. Learn to forgive yourself and others. Did you ever hear the expression, 'Women never forgive, men are too lazy to remember.' I think after awhile we have to let go of our grudges.

"But back to penance—our Christian faith tells us that we are ready to forgive ourselves. Don't carry self imposed guilt. I once heard someone say as he looked back. It was on old football player. He said, "I'd do everything the same way." Would I do

everything the same? I wish I could say that. One thing I would do differently, I would say I'm sorry to all those I hurt. And in many cases, I've let the time pass too long. Forgiveness and saying I'm sorry are two of the toughest things we are called to do. But nonetheless, I think this is part of the whole human learning curve. And becoming Christ-like means learning how to forgive and ask forgiveness."

~

TEACHING HIGH SCHOOL

"My 28 years of teaching were gratifying but I wouldn't consider myself a great teacher. I was able to present material well enough and I hope the students were learning something but the defining moment of my teaching years wasn't the teaching but the sacramental dimension of my priesthood. I was able to bring another dimension to the community I worked in and to individual students and teachers.

"I particularly was thankful that so many had asked me to officiate at their weddings and then of course the subsequent baptisms of their children. I'd be invited to family events and people included me as family so that meant an enormous amount to me. A student came up to me once and told me his father had died. I didn't know the student particularly well but he asked me to say the funeral Mass. We talked. He told me of his Dad and their relationship. I did the Mass but my point is that being a priest, being available to people in need, was more important than the teaching hours. When people—kids and adults—would stop me in the hallway and ask, 'Can you help me, can you talk to my parents, can you help me reconcile with my wife, visit my sick sister in the hospital?' That's what has defined my life and given deep meaning to my life as a priest.

"What I liked about teaching was the interaction with students. Sometimes the best part of teaching is when you're not con-

sciously teaching but getting off the subject. When you get off a topic, kids like to talk about their own lives, their fears, the pressures. I always saw this as an opportunity to put Christianity into their lives. Not smashing them over the head with it but suggesting an ideal. I propose the ideal, what Christ proposes. And then let them know that at times we all fall short, many times, we, me, and them. I hope they left with a sense of peace and security or at least there was some comfort in knowing their spiritual side. That was a big part of the job. Getting them in touch with that part of themselves.

"A graduate will come back and say, 'You influenced me.' That means to me that I had an impact on their life. And hopefully, the Church, their religion, or at least their spiritual self still means something. But there were a lot of kids I could never reach. Like one of St. Paul's letters. I couldn't be all things to all people. I just didn't have that ability. Some kids just didn't like me. OR as I prefer to say, there were more than a few that I never found the key to unlock them. Sometimes that bothers me. There were some that I failed or didn't get through to. But I have faith there was someone else out there who did have the key. That's the beauty of creation, that someone else has gifts you don't have and can work magic where you can't. It's a nice plan.

"Advice to parents from my teaching days? No magic pill. But like I said, just be consistent. The worst parents don't see the problem. They refuse to accept that there is a problem. The best parents I was around were the ones willing to acknowledge that there is a problem and are willing to go to any length to solve it. Perfect kids come from perfect parents' and there are none of those either. When I was in school, if I told mom or dad that something was wrong in school, they would automatically assume that we, the kids were wrong.

"*Later in my teaching, parents couldn't admit their son was wrong. Parents fail their kids when they say things like, "He couldn't do something like that." He can, will, and usually does. That's part of growing up. Parents' job is to guide them through that process, not shield them from it. My second to last semester, I met with these parents. The son had no completed homework assignments, took no tests, and the parents had ignored eight notices I had sent home (maybe they never got them). But with this information in hand they say to me, 'What can you do for my son to help him pass?' Your son failed because you failed. Know what your kids are doing and know who they're doing it with. And more important, know what they're not doing and why.*

"*Parents would lie to my face to defend themselves. They covered up so often; they can't face the bigger issues that come later. A certain amount of it is luck but there's a lot of skill. I used to think a lot of the times, I got away with things. I didn't get away with anything. My parents chose to turn a blind eye. They just knew when to come down and when to ignore certain things. They knew the type of kids they wanted us to be and then set out to do their part to make it happen. I always thought that the really bad kids with bad parents that I've encountered knew what they were doing. They were the least agreeable to hear your constructive advice. And that's too bad because I didn't have an agenda. Just to help them help their child.*"

PRAYER

BILL WAS A FERVENT ADVOCATE OF PRAYER AND CONVINCED ME THAT I SHOULD DO THE SAME. TO THIS DAY, HE GREATLY AFFECTED MY THOUGHTS AND PRACTICE AROUND PRAYER.

"I can't prove it to you; I do know my faith makes me better. I can tell you that's the way I consciously try to view the world; it helps me accept sometimes painful realities. When I get up I pray. What I pray for everyday is the strength to accept the way things are. And that I have gratitude. I live with an appreciation of the good things I have. There's one lesson I can say was hard earned. And if you struggle with it, then I say work on it. It helps to have a talk with God. Just a simple talk."

⤫

BEST SERMON?

<small>WHAT'S YOUR HALL OF FAME SERMON?</small>

"Preaching at my mother's funeral. That's when I felt the most connected. As far as preaching is concerned, anytime I can take a topic and personalize it, that which is most personal is most universal. If it pertains to me, and I feel deeply about it, then it probably pertains to others. This is the honor of preaching. Remember Christ said, 'Unless you become like little children…' Children realize they are dependent on other people. That's all preaching is about to me. Reminding ourselves that we are dependent on other people. We have to realize that we need others and God in our lives. Have you come this far by yourself? I don't think so."

CHAPTER 11

ADIEU AND
WORDS TO REMEMBER

Dear Bill,

Good news! I finished the book. It's not what we originally planned, but after lots of anxiety and procrastination, I finally delivered on my promise to you. I tried very hard to represent the truth of my experience with you, in particular those last two years when we opened up to one another and became friends. And now, I'd like to reflect a little to let you know exactly what lessons I learned from you.

When we began our discussions, I had lots of doubts. Restless and cynical, I asked you to defend most of the Catholicism I was raised with and all of the priesthood that you stood for and so fervently believed in. And today I ask, am I better off because of my relationship with you? Absolutely. Am I more confident of my place in the universe? Is my belief in God any more certain? Yes, on both accounts. How about my Christian principles? Stronger, more established? I hope so.

When I first asked you to participate in writing a book, I was only trying to help you pass some time in convalescence. However, subconsciously, and often consciously, I wanted answers from you. You were this larger-than-life person who had all the answers to life's most vexing question. I wanted a short cut to the Promised Land. Of course, that notion got thrown out in our very first meeting when you insisted, "I know nothing!" But it's been a few years since your death, and I've catalogued several important lessons you taught me that remain with me today.

BE REAL

When I think of you today, I think of the Velveteen Rabbit. I'm sure you remember the story. The rabbit learns what it means to be real. Bill, you were real. You had no pretense. You couldn't. At a young age you lost everything that was physical. With your accident and the resulting paralysis, the only thing you possessed was your real self, your essence. I remember your telling me that you weren't able to identify yourself by a variety of external roles that the rest of us do because most of your external choices were taken away.

As for myself, I've tried on far too many roles throughout my life. Even now, I catch myself acting at times, trying too hard to please or impress others, or to be something I'm not. In short, I fail to be authentic. I try too hard to be what others want me to be or I worry whether or not I'm liked. And then I'm hurt when significant people, whose opinions I value, aren't pleased with me. I've spent entirely too much time making myself worthy in the sight of others. Insecurity? That's what the experts would call it. Not being comfortable in one's own skin, trying to be something you're not? I think we can all admit to doing these things at some point in our lives.

But not you.

You knew who you were. You had nothing to impress others with except yourself. You were pleased and comfortable with yourself. One day you said something that still resonates in me:

> *"Know yourself and love that person. Not in an egotistical way but know that in God's eyes you're worthy and then bring love to others."*

You were teaching me to be authentic. To be true to myself and others. Nothing new. Not earth shattering. But nonetheless, you taught me well with your example. You taught me that when I strip everything away, all I have is my essence which makes me what I am. And I should bring the best of that to the world every day. Since your death, many of your quotes echo in my head, most often when I'm feeling down or trying to figure out the meaning of what the heck I'm doing here on earth. Do you remember that conversation we had where you spoke of the crisis of modernity. You spoke of how we live in the richest country in the history of mankind, yet we feel empty, lost, devoid of meaning. You were very adamant that we wouldn't find happiness in a bottle of booze or a bottle of pills. Your instruction was:

> *"Find peace with yourself. Don't search for happiness; look for understanding."*

You often spoke of life as a journey, and that no matter what one's position in life is, God gives us the tools to figure things out for ourselves. You told me many times that contentment came from living truthfully from my core. You explained,

> *"I had to shed everything and live with my true self and then learn to look at others in the same way."*

Your message always was to be honest with myself and let go of the illusions that others measure us with but seek to be a giver in life. You did three things consistently that I came to appreciate. You gave freely of yourself; you listened without judging; and you loved unconditionally. And your last quote on realness should be etched somewhere in stone,

> *"Love the life that God gave you."*

❧

REAL LOVE

You had one prized possession which you cherished. And you took it to the grave with you. Love.

> *"It's the only thing you get when you come into life and it's the only thing you take out of it, and I've had a lot of it,"* you once said.

Most people spend their lives searching for it. Many of us chase it, fail at it, or spend our time not knowing how to give or receive it. According to you, love was the only thing that you lived for.

"Without the love of my family and friends, I wouldn't have sur-
vived my accident," you assured me. "I would have died many
times if I didn't have them to live for."

Without the energy they brought to you, you could not have battled the
daily challenges you faced. Remember your last Christmas? We watched
Jimmy Stewart in *It's A Wonderful Life*. You confided to me that George
Bailey's experience was your exact experience at nineteen years of age.

"I knew that I was rich because I had family and friends who
loved me," you said.

It was a simple lesson but a great one—appreciation needs to be cultivated. That same day we talked about how it was difficult to be on the
receiving end of love when you feel you can't give back. You confessed
that you had to learn to receive love, "which may have been more difficult than giving love to others." In fact, you went on to explain,

"I had to learn that I was dependent on the kindness of others
and that took me a long time to accept and I couldn't pay any-
one back."

For myself, I admitted that I was guilty of giving out conditional love.
I came clean with the fact that I often attached conditions to niceness.
Even toward you, part of my early resentment centered on my perception that I should be appreciated for what I thought was my great kindness. Your coldness and aloofness got to me. Over the years, that need
of mine disappeared. Thank goodness you promised me that you understood where I was coming from and we cleared all that up.

"It's hard to admit those unpleasant things about ourselves, but
it's good to be honest about it," you said. We resolved that dis-
cussion by agreeing that the only thing you could give me back
was your time with me, and that was what we gave to each
other over the years.

As a listener, you were legendary and in my experience, unparalleled.
You could sit quietly, let me vent, never judging, and in the end, instruct

me that all would be well if I embraced God's love. I vividly remember one particular day I was hot blooded with anger with a co-worker. I cursed and spoke uncharitably about this person and what I'd like to say to him if I had the chance. You chuckled for a minute but then gently reminded me,

> *"Love him no matter what he did and you'll find peace; that's God's way. All of your anger is just going to make you sick. Give in to God's love, you'll be surprised what appears in your life."*

Like Mother Teresa, you were big on the notion that God spoke to us in those moments when we were our worst unloving selves. And God spoke to us through our enemies. Probably your most important message to me was that life was actually very, very simple.

> *"Love God by loving your neighbor, give and receive love is the big Christian message...the rest is just buildings and ceremonies,"* you instructed. *"Love is our pipeline to the divine and God's waiting for us to get that one of these days and in the meantime, he's being very patient with us."*

⌒⌒

BROKEN POTS

I know you used to give Don Burt credit for the "broken pots" metaphor, but it was one of our really memorable conversations. You often spoke of how each of us was placed here as "broken." I believe you attributed that to "original sin" and you had a great saying about ourselves,

> *"We often get rid of friends rather than examine ourselves."*

One of your great strengths as a person was that despite being near perfect in everyone else's estimation, you saw that you still had work to do on yourself. Once after I told you a story of a friend who wronged me, you laughed and corrected me for "spending a lot of time like Kojak, trying to pin the crime of being human on the other guy."

You taught me to approach relationships from my own brokenness. I, too, more than likely, was probably perceived by others to be the problem.

> *"Don't blame, accept…fix yourself before setting off to fix everyone else."*

Remember when I told you that I always thought the secret to happiness was to reduce one's expectations. You laughed. I think you actually wanted to agree but then you said,

> *"Let God work through others…listen…let Him work his magic."*

You were the least defensive person I've ever met. You always began the conversation taking responsibility for your own imperfection. That kind of humility impacted me greatly and your humble aura still surrounds me.

⌘

WAITING

You waited for everything. From the first moments after your accident, you were doomed to a life of waiting. There wasn't one single task that you could do without assistance. A minor itch or major headache required the assistance of another. Always waiting. Waiting for a family member, a friend, or a stranger to remember,

"Oh, Bill needs some help."

This is no doubt the most significant lesson I received from you—Herculean patience in the face of forever bouts of waiting. Your example was something I'll treasure to my grave, but your common sense words should be required reading for anyone trying to learn how to live this thing we call life. The first thing you told me about patience was,

> *"I'm God's poster boy for teaching you don't get what you want, but God sends what you need."*

You were a throwback guy, like those old World War II images when men were rugged, strong, and silent. You were impatient with the modern, spoiled American who wanted quick results and fast pleasure. The only people you openly criticized were any folks with an "I want it now" attitude. You believed that the most effective lesson we need to consider is the lesson of waiting.

As a parent, I've often used you as an example when I was explaining to my children the very difficult explanation of delayed gratification. Not only did you show me the importance of "good things come to those who wait," you also taught that patience was not only in the waiting but also in the trusting of life and God's plan. You spoke to me many times about the problems of control and our tendency to want to have the upper hand on every outcome.

> *"Even in my wheelchair, with this paralyzed body, I've learned that it still works out," you said. "Things work out in God's time, not yours and don't forget, God only gives you what he thinks you can handle," was another quote you spilled out. "I had to learn to practice patience," you admitted.*

Surprisingly, I discovered that secretly you harbored some resentment when you had to wait on what you called, "stupidity." You had an impatient side, and I felt the sting a few times but later I realized that I was guilty of glaring stupidity in my lackadaisical care of you. Even the Christ-like Father Atkinson had to develop his patience muscles.

> *"It's one of the jobs we have to do, and if you pay attention to developing patience, you'll survive the really difficult times as well as helping others around you to do the same."*

It was the one thing about yourself that you were proud to brag about.

> *"Yes, I probably am one of the most patient people you'll meet."*

Yes, you were.

"WATCH FOR THE ILLUSION OF POWER"

You played your cards very close to your vest. You weren't one for criticizing others or talking about people. In fact, I never once heard you openly criticize a fellow priest by name, and if memory serves me right, I never heard an uncharitable word leave your lips. You would allow me to do the dirty work and then laugh at my frustrations. I am not like you. I'm tough on others. So being around you was often like going to the optometrist. You helped correct my poor vision. However, without using names, you did rail at a certain type of individual. You were never impressed with people who pursued power and wealth. You told me,

> *"I'll never understand even my own Augustinian brothers who seem to chase power through ambition or position."*

You were not impressed easily with a person's résumé or their bank account. Your advice to me in my moments of self-doubt was,

> *"Your inner strength and your integrity, that's what counts in the eyes of God. He made you, he knows you, and he's not impressed with your bank account either but only the love with which you live by."*

You taught external power is not power at all but only a temporary fix for what ails us. Trying to control life or others leads us away from God's intentions for us. Your life was all about letting go of control because you learned the hard way that you had none. All of your power came from within. You credited your faith for this gift.

"LETTING GO"

WHAT WAS IT LIKE TO LOSE EVERYTHING THAT YOU HAD?" THAT WAS ONE OF THE FIRST QUESTIONS I EVER ASKED YOU ABOUT BECOMING A QUADRIPLEGIC. YOU ANSWERED ME IN AN ALMOST COCKY, SELF ASSURED WAY SAYING,

> *"We're all losing something all the time."*

I chuckled nervously at that time, and gave a perfunctory, "I guess so," but you frequently returned to this theme in our conversations, emphasizing the temporal nature of our lives. You scoffed when people felt sorry for your loss when, like me, they failed to contemplate their own. Learning to understand and deal with the fact of loss in all of our lives was one of your "greatest hits." You believed that we're all on a rapidly advancing journey and nothing that comes our way do we get to keep. Whether it is our physical bodies or our loved ones, we're going to experience loss. But you also assured me, with this loss, God steps in and gives us the love of family, friends, and very often perfect strangers.

> *"I lost my independence," you calmly told me, "but people like yourself showed up…I can bemoan the loss or I can be grateful for the assistance." And you were always true to that attitude.*

Initially, I believe I was more angry than you when I asked,

> "HOW ABOUT ALL YOUR DREAMS OF YOUTH; WHERE'D THEY GO?"

Your reply was simply,

> *"It's all just temporary and my dreams just had to change."*

One thing that amazed me was that essentially you lived entirely two lives. You had to bury that nineteen-year-old kid and rise up into a new reality. Most of us never learn the lesson of impermanence. We search, we crave, and we so hope for a security that promises we can hold on to everything. We want to keep things always the same. But you dealt so frequently with dying that you never kidded yourself. You knew you were only one short breath away from the last loss.

Myself, I am one of those people who resist the notion of change. I'm saddened when someone close to me is taken away, especially someone like yourself. I'd like some of those days back when we just seemed to be clicking. Without a doubt, this was the toughest of all lessons for me. You made me realize that the good times don't last forever, but neither do the bad times. Things do change. Life is lost, second by second. My earliest memories of my parents were the lessons of appreciating what I had. That's easier said than done. Somehow, human nature, being what it is, we try to deny the inevitable that we know to be true. As a parent today, I'm boring my children with the same clichés. Be happy for what you have; don't waste your life wanting things you don't need. Will they ever get that concept? Yes, they will—if they meet a great teacher like I did.

⁓

FINALLY!

I know this letter is really long, Bill, but just a few more thoughts, and I'll be on my way; my promise to you fulfilled at last. I know you're present somewhere—right at this very moment. I feel your presence. That's a big thing for me to finally admit. And so, wherever you are, I hope you can read or feel this. Since there's no time/space continuum, the good thing for you is that my long-winded message can be read in an instant, freeing you up to do other things.

Your entire life was a preparation to meet God, face-to face. That was one of the last things you told me. I felt relieved, though, when you admitted that for most of your life, you, like me, you did fear death. But in the last year of your life, you abandoned that fear and embraced peace instead. That's what I remember most about our last few times together. You no longer fought life but calmly let whatever was going to happen, happen. The big lesson you showed me was letting go and trusting in whatever came your way. You drew comfort in the faith that you were going someplace better, and I'm very much hoping you arrived in that place and you've been reunited with your old mobile self again.

Thank you for the examples you gave me. Your insistence on following "Thy Will" rather than "my will" is just one lesson I will try to emulate always. Your other lessons included: living in the moment, living with courage, and living with the knowledge that we must constantly go with life's flow and adapt. They were all empty clichés to me until you showed me how these "clichés" take real live commitment to achieve. You taught me true perspective and not to whine. Very important in my life today. You let me in on your suffering and taught me that even with the worst that life throws at you, you can create the silver lining. God knows I did enough whining to you, but you always responded with patience and understanding—gifts I cherish even today. Most of all you taught me that a happy life was seeded with gratitude. When we first met, I didn't think you had much to be grateful for and everything to be bitter about. I learned that joy comes from the simplest choices. Choosing love over hate, possibility over lamentation, and hope over despair are autographs you carved on my memory.

Bill, you lived a most successful life. Like Job, you weathered the toughest storms life could muster. When God appeared to turn away from you, you patiently waited for an answer from Him. You took a nightmare and used it as fodder for deep wisdom. And like every great hero, you reluctantly and humbly shared it with the rest of us.

My prayer to you today is to continue to be present to us and guide us through this mystery we find ourselves in every day. Help us to wake up each day with an appreciation for all that we have been given. Help us to see purpose on cloudy days. And for the world? Well, as far as I'm concerned, you're a saint now, right? So I can officially ask you to intercede with God on our behalf.

So how about a little world peace?

Thanks dear friend!

Steve

February 2nd, 1974 – on the day of Bill's ordination at St. Alice's Church.
On the left is Bill's brother, Allen Atkinson, Father Bill Atkinson and
Father John Melton, OSA (Bill's counselor at Msgr. Bonner High School).
This was almost nine years after the accident that left Bill a quadriplegic.

CHAPTER 12

EPILOGUE AND REMINISCENCES

F ATHER BILL ATKINSON WAS A FORCE OF NATURE; AS A YOUTH, HIS FAMILY HAD thought he or his brother might become a sporting "star."

The *Fates* play strange games with us all and with none more so than the Atkinson boys. Bill became a commited priest tethered to a quadriplegic's chair. Al became a star football player who joined Joe Namath and the New York Jets to become the "giant killers" who soundly beat the heavily favored Baltimore Colts in Super Bowl III.

To his family and friends, Bill also became a "giant killer" who beat back the demons which could have entered his soul after a split-second mistake sent his toboggan careening into a tree on a snow-covered New York hill. Any of us would surely cry "Why me? What did I do to deserve this?" That is human nature—and Bill surely had moments of doubt, moments of self-pity—but, Life offers no pity; it demands that we go on, or give in and perish. Bill followed a glorious path to self-realization, humility, forgiveness and service to his fellow man. He gave more than he took but he was ever conscious of what his family and friends gave to him. There was much discomfort in having to accept so much help, with a feeling that he could never repay the goodness of others.

As Steve McWilliams ran home to his wife after so many years of silent days with Bill, and joyfully exclaimed "He asked me to come over and watch a game," that enthusiastic joy was not witnessed by Bill Atkinson, but is adequate testament that he was not "taking" from others, but providing joy to others when simply offering himself.

The following pages allow others to express what "Father Bill" meant to them and we have included some photographs so that you, dear reader, can share some more intimate moments and thoughts about this holy and humble man.

—PAUL NIGEL HARRIS, PUBLISHER
12TH AUGUST, 2011

"Here's a side bar memory on Bill but my story includes his mother, Mary. 'Mrs. A' as I called her, was an incredible woman and she was the real strength of the family. When she was dying (we had become very good friends), Bill was being ordained a deacon. I asked her if what she had been doing all these years (after Bill's accident) was offering her life for Bill. She said 'Yes.' I said, 'You know that God has taken you seriously don't you?' She replied, 'Yes.' She had just gotten out of the hospital in 1965 from having a breast removed for cancer when Bill had the accident. At Bill's ordination, a television newswoman stuck a microphone in Bill's face and said, 'Isn't it too bad your mother couldn't be here?' Mrs. A had died before the ordination. In fact, Bill had preached at her funeral…Back to the newswoman: Bill looked at her with his wry smile and said, 'Oh, I don't know, I think she had the best seat in the house!' "

—FATHER ART CHAPPELL, OSA, FELLOW AUGUSTINIAN

Young Bill Atkinson begins his religious quest
flanked by his proud parents, Al and Mary Atkinson

After his accident and extensive rehabilitation, Bill Atkinson returned to his "normal" life but he was now totally dependent on others. Here, with his father and mother he dines and drinks with the help of his dad—who is proud of and awed by the strength and resilience of his young son.

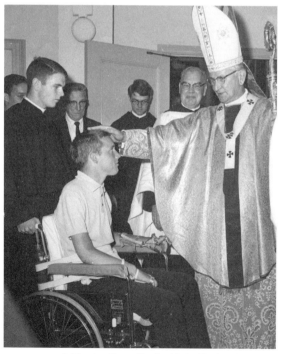

A Blessing from Cardinal John Krol

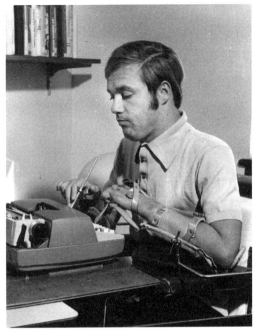

In the Fall of 1966 Bill began his studies at
Villanova University at St. Mary's Hall.
This photo is from the late 1960s.

"The man is a saint. He handled every cross God put down
in front of him with love. Love of God and love of those who
helped him and for all those who need him. He listened but
never judged. He advised, when asked, but never admon-
ished. I learned from Bill to try and stop complaining.
Complaining about what God has or has not done. Bill
taught me to accept, to deal and to work through life's dif-
ficulties with dignity.

—ELLEN DELANEY, LONGTIME FRIEND

Bill returned to the seminary in 1966
after a year at Magee Rehabilitation Hospital in Philadephia

Bill enjoys a meal with friends at the Villanova University dining hall

Bill the Novitiate at St. Thomas of Villanova

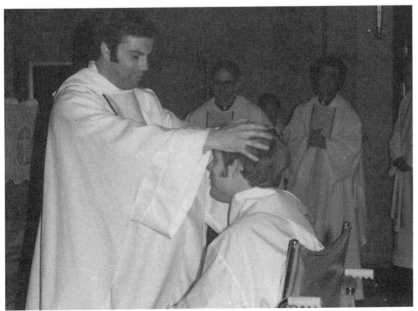

Art Chappell lays his hands on the head of Bill Atkinson;
Art was in seminary with Bill at the time of his toboggan accident

"The Heron and Atkinson families have been friends for as long as I remember. Bill was a year below me in school but we were altar boys together and we played baseball together. Bill was always a shy person but a really nice guy...Years after the accident, Bill was later ordained a priest and his first assignment was as a teacher at Monsignor Bonner High School. While living at Bonner, Bill developed decubitis ulcers, which are painful bed sores. He had to return to Magee Rehab for treatment. I went to visit him at Magee and being a nurse, I asked him if he had help with daily care. He advised that he was assisted by his fellow Augustinians who resided with him at the time. It became apparent that additional nursing care was needed. It was at this point (1976) that Bill and I began our nurse/patient relationship.

"When I first started to be on Bill's team of caregivers, he had already established his way of doing things even if it didn't measure up to my strict nursing procedures. I quickly learned that Bill liked to keep things simple and not complicated. He didn't believe in buying all the latest medical equipment and supplies. He would purchase glass syringes and stainless steel bowls so that they could be sterilized in boiling water and not have to be replaced after each use. An early enviromentalist! Bill had a routine to his daily living...Little did I realize that saying 'yes' to providing nursing care in 1976 would turn into a 30-year friendship. Being a part of Bill's life on a daily basis was not a hardship but an opportunity for me to use my talents to help another person in need.

"When I was in the 7th grade and in the Boy Scouts, a group of us went on a camping trip. During the night a thunderstorm came up and our tent was struck by lightning. Several of us were seriously injured and one of the boys died. It was a tragic experience for us. When I came home from the hospital, I had to spend a lot of time resting on the living room couch because my muscles had been damaged. One day, a priest from our parish, Father Kearney came to visit me. He told my mother that God had protected me because He had other plans for me. My mother later told me that I had been spared so I might care for Bill.

"I believe that Bill allowed his devastating accident and life as a quadriplegic to enable him to be a better person and a true Christian. In some ways I think that through the years his experiences allowed him to be a 'mystic.' His time spent in meditation and contemplation gave him an 'intuition' and a sense of spirituality that was so unique to Bill. At the same time he was a 'regular guy.' He wasn't a holy roller or someone 'in your face' about his faith....You learned about real spirituality by just being with Bill, watching him, talking with him, seeing how he interacted with others in everyday situations.

"Bill loved to play practical jokes on people, especially his students. For example, he might send a postcard from some exotic location to a graduate and sign someone else's name. Eventually the kid would figure out it was from Father Bill.

"I learned many things from Bill. Some of the important things are to enjoy the moment and the simple things in life. He loved just sitting in the sun and feeling the warm rays on his face. He never felt as though he needed a lot of 'things.' If he hadn't used something in a year, he figured it was time to get rid of it. If he had read a book, he would give it away for someone else to enjoy. Being a quadriplegic, Bill learned to be patient—really patient! He needed people to help him with every function in life.

He was a dear friend and I miss him.

—RICHARD HERON, NURSE

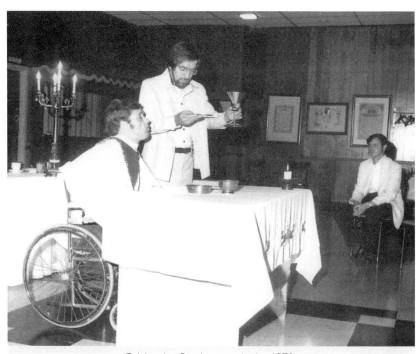

Celebrating Sunday mass in the 1970s
at Knights of Columbus in Springfield, (Delaware County, PA)
with the help of his good friend Rich Heron as Don Smith looks on

1973 Bill with his mother and father – Bill was now a Deacon

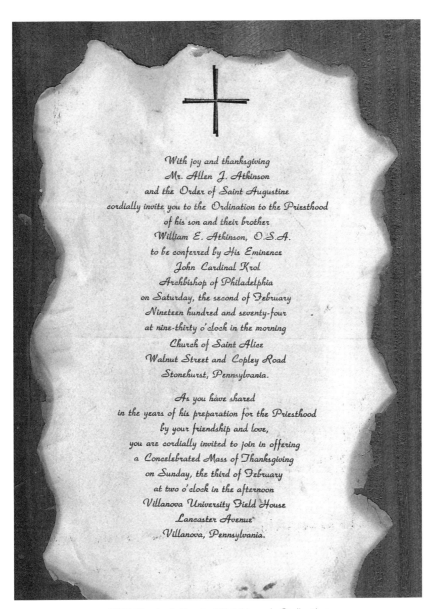

With joy and thanksgiving
Mr. Allen J. Atkinson
and the Order of Saint Augustine
cordially invite you to the Ordination to the Priesthood
of his son and their brother
William E. Atkinson, O.S.A.
to be conferred by His Eminence
John Cardinal Krol
Archbishop of Philadelphia
on Saturday, the second of February
Nineteen hundred and seventy-four
at nine-thirty o'clock in the morning
Church of Saint Alice
Walnut Street and Copley Road
Stonehurst, Pennsylvania.

As you have shared
in the years of his preparation for the Priesthood
by your friendship and love,
you are cordially invited to join in offering
a Concelebrated Mass of Thanksgiving
on Sunday, the third of February
at two o'clock in the afternoon
Villanova University Field House
Lancaster Avenue
Villanova, Pennsylvania.

1974 The Invitation to Bill Atkinson's Ordination

Feb 2nd, 1974 – Bill with Cardinal Krol on the day of his Ordination

Feb 2nd, 1974 - Bill with his father & grandmother at St. Alice's Parish

"Father Atkinson was a remarkable man, an inspirational leader, a great priest, and a wonderful friend and mentor to countless students. There isn't a more beloved figure on the Monsignor Bonner and Archbishop Prendergast campus than Father Atkinson, even to this day. It is my hope that those who read this book will experience something of Father Atkinson's love of God and humanity and that by keeping his memory and legacy close to our hearts, we ourselves will become better people."

—FATHER JAMES OLSON, PRESIDENT
MONSIGNOR BONNER & ARCHBISHOP PRENDERGAST HIGH SCHOOL

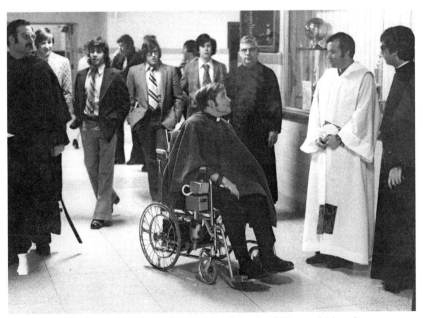

Whether at Monsignor Bonner High School or Villanova University,
"Father Bill" was a familiar sight in his cloak

"Father Bill made me the teacher that I am. He urged me to quit teaching if I ever stopped caring. He taught me that sometimes a good lesson does not involve the subject we teach but the humanity that we share with our students. By his every day example, he showed me that we can chose to focus on the things that we cannot do and cannot have or we can focus on the things we can do and have. He chose to live for years though there were times he could have chosen to let go. He showed me what the love of God looks like in someone who has not gotten everything handed to him on a silver platter. He showed me acceptance…He accepted me the way I was . I think the most amazing thing that he taught me was not with words. I don't even know if I can use words to describe it. Everyone I know has a cross to carry, most small, some large, and many inconsequential. Yet, everyone who needed to vent about those crosses flew to Father like moths to flames. He listened, consoled, sometimes not giving advice but just soothing sentiments. Sometimes he just stated the obvious but always encouraging the person and offering his prayers. Yet most of the time, 95%, people brought him things much smaller than the everyday trials he lived. Imagine not being able to open your own mail, feed yourself, get out of bed without the constant presence of someone else, and in the end having to trust in a breathing machine to keep him sustained, and then listen to me complain that my basement flooded or I was having a bad day. I think he taught me that people need to feel that their problems are important, and they need someone to take their problems to, and in the end he reminded me of what God must be like. Always listening to our daily gripes, never saying, I'm tired of listening to your petty problems. Always asking, how can I help? That was the biggest lesson!"

—KATIE CAMPBELL, TEACHER, MONSIGNOR BONNER HIGH SCHOOL

In his signature hat, with his "game face" set, Father Bill eagerly
anticipates another great performance by the Bonner team!

Inducted into the Monsignor Bonner High School "Hall of Fame"...
behind Father Bill are his brother, Al Atkinson, and Father John Melton

Bill loved his time with family at the "Jersey Shore"

Bill with his good friends Frank and Maggie Riley and his father, Al Atkinson

1992 Ed, Mary (Fr. Bill's cousin) and Joe Moody with Bill at Ed's high school graduation from St. James. Ed was the first family member Bill baptized after his ordination.

1997 A Christmas photo at Joan Alice and John Mullen's home.
His sister Joan Alice and his entire family provided undying support for Father Bill.

Bill and his siblings — BACK: Ed Atkinson, Mary D'Allesandro, Betty Harvey, Al Atkinson, Jr.. FRONT: Pat McCaffrey, Father Bill Atkinson, Joan Mullen

2005 Bill with his night nurse and angel, Mary Brady, who soothed and comforted him during those long, sleepless nights in Ocean City, NJ – here they took a short visit to the boardwalk...possibly his last.

Two Great Men Meet:
Father Bill Atkinson, OSA meets Pope John Paul II.
Pope Paul VI had given his blessing to Bill becoming a priest thus allowing him to serve
his fellow man for so many decades. As Cardinal Krol noted when Bill became a priest,
this young man had so much to give...pity never entered the decision...Father Bill
was expected to work hard and serve...and that he did...like few before him.

Father Bill Atkinson, OSA

"A resounding question that was always posed to Bill was, 'How do you do it?' And his answer was always the same. 'A lot of people wouldn't let me die. I could never have done it by myself, and so it goes, nobody does it by themselves. It must be done by others. Without them I couldn't have done it.'"

—JOAN ALICE ATKINSON MULLEN
(FROM BILL'S EULOGY, 19TH SEPTEMBER, 2006)